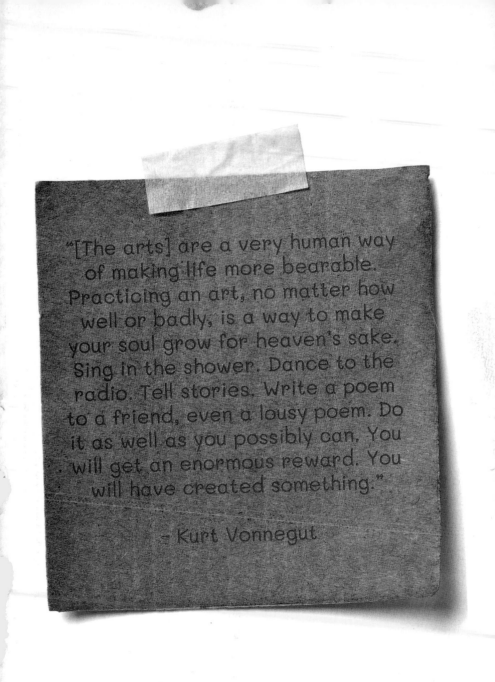

"[The arts] are a very human way of making life more bearable. Practicing an art, no matter how well or badly, is a way to make your soul grow for heaven's sake. Sing in the shower. Dance to the radio. Tell stories. Write a poem to a friend, even a lousy poem. Do it as well as you possibly can. You will get an enormous reward. You will have created something."

– Kurt Vonnegut

Brian Solis

WILEY

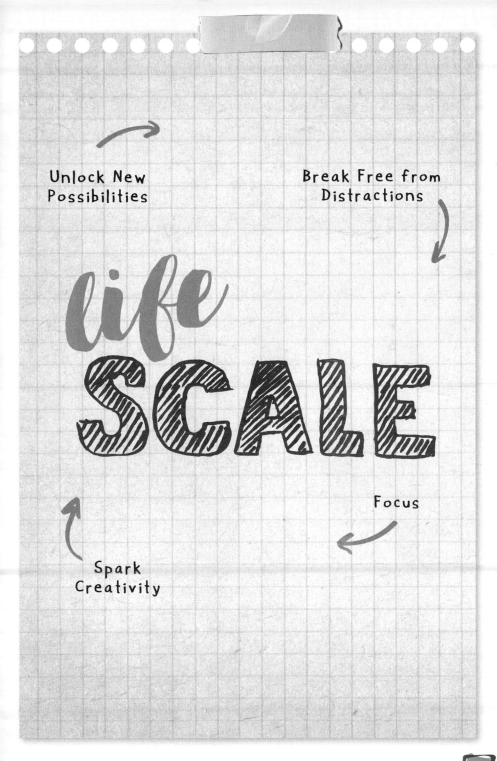

Unlock New
Possibilities

Break Free from
Distractions

life

SCALE

Focus

Spark
Creativity

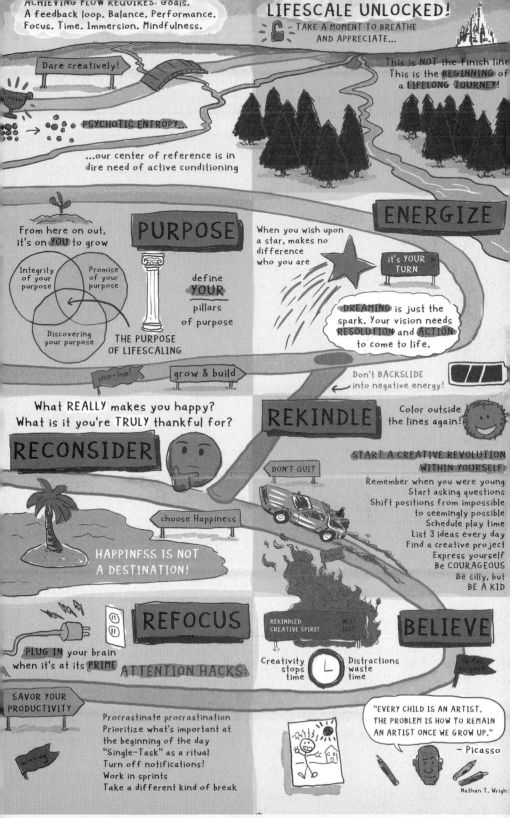

For general information on our other products and services or for technical support, please contact our Customer Care Department within the United States at (800) 762-2974, outside the United States at (317) 572-3993 or fax (317) 572-4002.

Wiley publishes in a variety of print and electronic formats and by print-on-demand. Some material included with standard print versions of this book may not be included in e-books or in print-on-demand. If this book refers to media such as a CD or DVD that is not included in the version you purchased, you may download this material at http:// booksupport.wiley.com. For more information about Wiley products, visit www.wiley.com.

ISBN 9781119535867 (Hardcover)
ISBN 9781119535874 (ePDF)
ISBN 9781119535850 (ePub)

Cover design: Briana Schweizer

Lifescale journey illustration and font: Nathan T. Wright

Printed in the United States of America

V10007730 012219

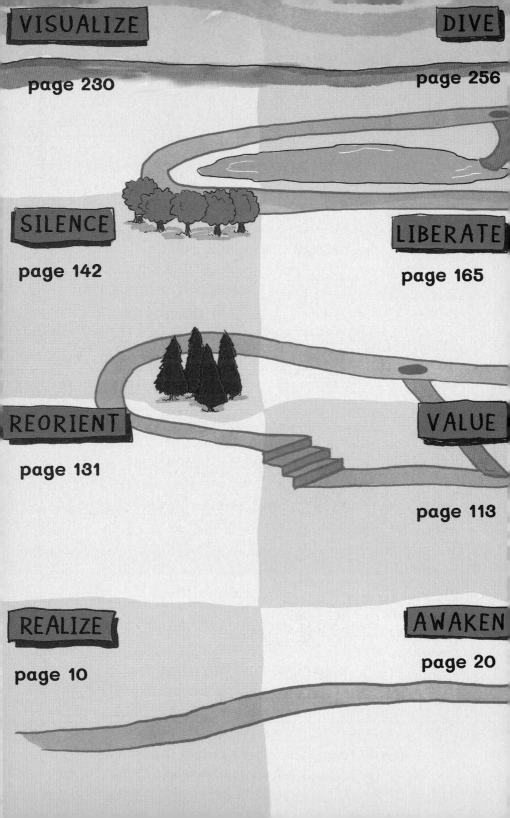

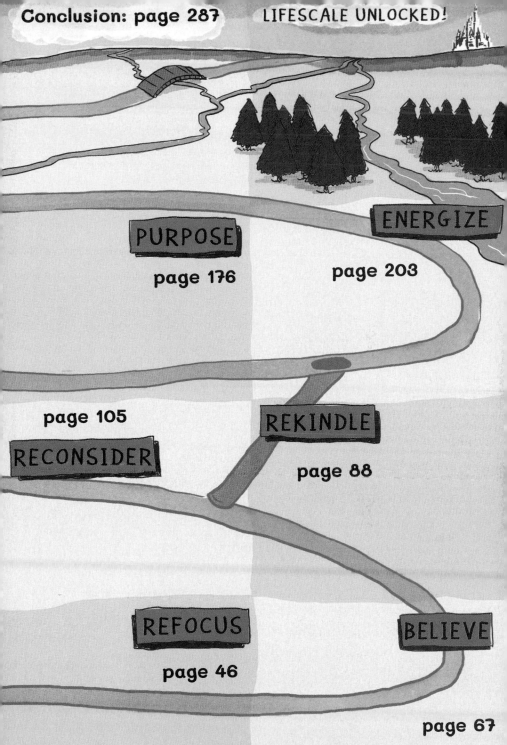

REALIZE

"Your vision will become clear
only when you can look into your own heart. Who looks
outside, dreams; who looks inside, awakes."

– Carl Jung

I'm still not sure exactly when I first realized I had a problem.

I began to notice that I couldn't focus the way I used to. I felt on edge often and I wasn't having much fun at all, constantly puting off "me" time and time with friends and family to keep up with commitments. I was almost always either online or on my phone, needlessly consuming content with no real bearing on either my personal or work lives.

Diving deep into topics for my research had become increasingly difficult, and I couldn't sit still and read a book for more than 10 or 15 minutes, whereas losing myself in a book used to be a great joy. I kept forgetting about important events coming up, and found myself making lots of careless little mistakes. I would also catch myself staring at a screen or talking at people when I was in meetings or out with friends more than listening.

I had everything in check . . . or, so I thought. I was still getting things done. I was cranking through to-do lists. I was producing. I was studying and learning. I couldn't see yet that everything took much longer than it should or that the output

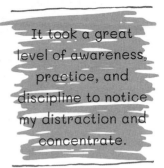

It took a great level of awareness, practice, and discipline to notice my distraction and concentrate.

was only a small reflection of what was possible. I didn't see that other important missions and relationships were languishing.

As I became more and more distracted, I had to work hard to catch myself in the acts of swerving away from what I was doing or trying to accomplish, and then deliberately stop and force myself to re-center. The same was true for conversations or studying or reading. It took a great level of awareness, practice, and discipline to notice my distraction and concentrate.

Yet I only began to take a serious look at what was happening when I sat down to write the proposal for what was initially going to be my next book. One year later, I shelved the project. Though I'm still devastated about it, I learned something about myself in the process that led me to write this other book, to this moment with you.

After I closed the chapter on my previous book, I couldn't wait to imagine new possibilities, to pursue another dimension of creativity . . . to learn, experiment, and push the boundaries of what books could be and how we interact with them. The romance of my last creative affair ensnared me and unlocked a desire for not only another similar liaison, but also for something deeper and even

Realize

more impassioned. It took just over two years to officially embrace the fact that the time had come to create something new.

> My ability to imagine and think critically was fractured and fragmented.

I not only took longer between projects, but when I finally sat down to explore the depths of my next idea, I struggled. I froze. Something was different. Ideation was limited and quite honestly, average. I thought "Maybe it's just cobwebs." That's partially true. I noticed more problems, however. I couldn't dive as deep as I used to. My ability to imagine and think critically was fractured and fragmented. When I finally, FINALLY reached creative depths, I couldn't stay there for long without coming up for distractions that would, for some strange reason, serve as oxygen.

Rather than stepping back to reflect and analyze, I tried harder. I became anxious about everything, even the simplest of projects, which triggered procrastination and avoidance. Over time, my penchant for procrastination became pronounced. It was just a given and instead of understanding the cause, I learned the phases of working around and through it. But ultimately, my activity shifted to bursts instead of solid streams. My to-do list was only focused on what was absolutely due, while everything else languished, which, I learned, causes an entirely different level of anxiety. The more items reside on the list, the more stress they cause by just sitting there. It didn't matter. I had become a "fireman" putting out only burning fires and always planning to focus on, but really never getting to, other (less) critical tasks.

> "Next time you're afraid to share ideas, remember someone once said in a meeting, 'Let's make a film with a tornado full of sharks.'"

I berated and questioned myself. I was losing self-esteem. And as my confidence and creativity deflated, I started to realize that my happiness was also fading. I just couldn't identify or admit it in the moment. I couldn't exactly pinpoint what was happening or why.

Then one day I was struggling to complete an article titled "How to Focus While Being Distracted," and the irony hit me, *hard*. I was totally distracted, being drawn to notification after notification from Snapchat, Facebook, Messenger, Instagram, WhatsApp, and Twitter. I'd tell myself not to reach for my phone, but there I'd be checking out a picture of that funny sandwich board outside of one of my friends favorite cafés that read, "Next time you're afraid to share ideas, remember someone once said in a meeting, 'Let's make a film with a tornado full of sharks.'" Ha, ha, ha!!

After a year of emotionally and intellectually treading water, I pressed pause. Not only was I afraid that I was losing my creative spark, I feared that I was losing touch with my ability to feel happiness. I realized that I was constantly postponing pursuit of my most significant dreams and aspirations, and I felt that I was actually losing the idea of who I really am, and want to be. All of my distraction was preventing me from living as I truly found meaningful.

Realize

When I shared this story with loved ones, so many of them shared tales of similar experiences. That's when I realized that I needed to look for answers, for myself, for them, and for you too.

Ask yourself, when did:

We get so busy?

Being glued to our devices get normalized?

It get so difficult to focus or stay focused?

We decide constant multitasking was in our best interests?

Consuming everyone else's life become more important than actually living our lives?

We start to feel all of this nonstop anxiety?

When did it get so hard to breathe?

We started consuming more than we were creating. We traded expression and imagination for scrolls and swipes. We were intoxicated by the blurring of life between physical and digital.

Every day we do our best to navigate life and keep up with our personal and professional responsibilities, but at the end of each day, we're still fighting to complete our self-imposed to-do lists, both at work and at home, a hamster-wheel process that detracts from our longer-term goals and dreams.[1]

A sort of Zombie Apocalypse has quietly crept up to our doorsteps.

I've seen it with my own eyes, you see it everywhere (when you happen to look up), dozens of people of all ages, impervious to traffic and the risk to their own lives, crossing the street glued to their phones. In New York, for example, thousands of teens end up in the emergency room every year thanks to traffic accidents caused by mobile distraction.

Around the world, urban planners are rethinking crosswalk design to prevent this type of thing from happening, while sidewalks in China now have designated cell phone lanes.

© Edwin Tanning, HIG

© Barcroft Media via Telegraph

Realize

Every day, we're finding it harder to disconnect, if we're trying to disconnect at all. Yet, every part of our lives is being disrupted. We're suffering from thinning attention spans, reduced empathy, narrowed inputs for intellectual and creative guidance and inspiration, diminished capacity for critical thinking, deep focus and creativity.

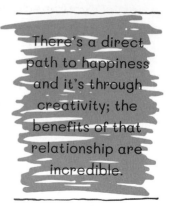

There's a direct path to happiness and it's through creativity; the benefits of that relationship are incredible.

All of our toggling between apps, networks, email, and texts comes at a tremendous cost to the actual work we're meant to be doing. Did you know that a significant share of the U.S. workforce spends two hours or more checking their smartphone at work every day? That adds up to at least 10 hours every week taken away from performing their jobs. Ten years ago, the average person, shifted attention every three minutes. Now, employees will last a whole 45 seconds before shifting their focus. What's more, today's average employee will check email 74 times a day and switch tasks on their computer 566 times per day. Additionally, when people are stressed, "they tend to shift their attention more rapidly," according to Dr. Mark. "So, we're in this vicious, habitual cycle."[2]

To get a sense of how much time you're spending with distractions, count, in just one day, how many times you...

Reach for a device

Check messages (total of all the messaging apps)

Check your feeds for updates

Share an experience or moment or simply a picture of yourself

Switch between any of the above and your work

Each time we waste time by falling into rabbit holes of digital distraction, we're paying an opportunity cost. And we're not just losing time we could invest better elsewhere, we are teaching ourselves that it's okay to waste time. Meanwhile, not only is our distraction eroding our productivity, it's undermining our mental health and well-being, inducing stress, anxiety, loneliness, low self-esteem and depression.[3]

Yet, through social media, we share an upbeat slice of our lives that gives everyone the impression we're happy and thriving, seamlessly balancing work and family, ambitious goals and adventurous leisure. The irony is that when we're not just posturing on social media, we're compelling the people who follow us to feel like they're not measuring up. Little do they know, however, we aren't actually living our best life, just a semblance of it. Deep down, we're not happy.

We keep telling ourselves we're fine—there's nothing to see here folks! We'll get to our hopes and dreams one day! But they seem to be gaining distance from us. We're also not as happy or as creative as we could be. And, those two things are interlinked . . . happiness and creativity.

We keep telling ourselves we're fine! We'll get to our hopes and dreams one day!

Realize

17

There's a direct path to happiness and it's through creativity; the benefits of that relationship are incredible. Your life at work, home, school, your side hustle, your relationships all greatly profit from your ability to devote time to thinking creatively.

This book isn't a rant about our relationship with technology. It's a guide to re-centering our minds and souls, freeing ourselves of the barrage of distractions and rekindling our creativity.

After two decades of promoting the virtues and promise of disruptive technology, I found myself at a crossroads. I could either continue dedicating my time to visualizing optimistic and productive scenarios for the future technology will bring—slowly and painfully as that work was going—or I could shift my focus to unraveling what was going wrong, for me and so many others, and how to get back on a healthy track.

I could only make one decision.

If ignorance is bliss, awareness is awakening. I realized that I needed to learn why I was falling prey to distraction; and to build new skills for focusing and tapping my creativity. I had to learn to build a buffer against the ever-evolving set of detractors, and to unlearn bad habits. And in order to truly revive my creative productivity, I also needed to reassess what I truly valued and dissect my own happiness and how I defined it. I set out to get my creativity and my happiness back, and I went on a journey of discovery. Along the way, I learned how to build a constructive new regimen, involving powerful creative habits, and to raise my self-awareness so that I could stick to that new life routine.

I call the method I developed for charting and staying on this new focused and productively creative course lifescaling; it's a process for achieving an intentional state of happiness, creativity and mastery in the face of the onslaught of distractions. Lifescaling isn't just about performance, it's about finding authentic happiness through unleasing your creativity, and about defining your own path in life, your own way.

The first step in lifescaling is coming to terms with why we've become so addicted to distraction. It's certainly not entirely our fault—not by a long shot—but the truth is that we've been complicit. So let's start by investigating why.

If ignorance is bliss, awareness is awakening

Realize

AWAKEN

The Gift of Awareness Is a Gift We First Give Ourselves, then Everyone Else

"Raise your awareness and share
your uniqueness to the world."
– Amit Ray

©Jacob Ufkes

Digital distraction is not something we were prepared for. Generations of education, parenting, management, and absorbing everyday ethics and norms couldn't have prepared us for the onslaught of information, showers of attention, celebration of self-interest and selfishness, and the flooding of egocentric emotions.

We didn't mean to become addicted. As with cigarettes in the early days, we didn't understand that our digital indulgences were made to be addictive, and we didn't have information about the health effects—on our bodies, emotions, and psyches.

Awaken

The Path to Distraction: How Did We Get Here?

> Our attention is traded as a commodity and the more of it we spend on any given platform or device, the more these hosts can sell it for.

I'm sure you have sometimes caught yourself in the mindless pattern of an "endless scroll," where you, without even thinking, scrolled and scrolled and scrolled, viewing and reacting to content, not because you wanted to, but because you couldn't help yourself. There's a reason for that.

As a geek apologist who championed Web 2.0, social media, and mobile apps, I was a hopeless optimist. Through my work I advised organizations, governments, institutions, and individuals on ways to best use these technologies for good. Over time, however, novices, opportunists, spammers, scammers, and eventually, villains, found insidious ways to gobble up our attention and capitalize on it. Some intentionally, and others unintentionally, exploited discoveries about how we could be manipulated to spend more and more time with their enticements.

Mark Zuckerberg, Steve Jobs, Twitter founders Evan Williams and Jack Dorsey, Snapchat founder Evan Spiegal, and the other leaders of web innovation played an intentional and influential role in capitalizing on human vulnerabilities. There are two ways to readily influence behavior: (1) manipulate it or (2) inspire it. The technology companies have chosen, for the most part, to manipulate it.

The attention economy has been wildly lucrative. No wonder; our attention is finite, which creates limited supply and great demand. Netflix CEO Reed Hastings once said the company's number one competitor was sleep. "And, we're winning!" he proudly exclaimed to shareholders.[1] The attention economy is no mere metaphor; our attention is traded as a commodity and the more of it we spend on any given platform or device, the more those hosts can sell it for.

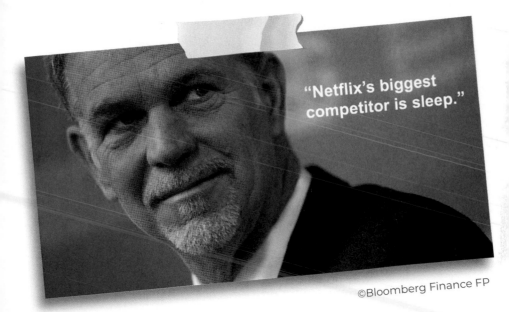

"Netflix's biggest competitor is sleep."

©Bloomberg Finance FP

Justin Rosenstein, one of the four Facebook designers behind the "Like" button, explained the potential and danger of social rewards in an interview with *Vice*.[2]

"The main intention I had was to make positivity the path of least resistance. And I think it succeeded in its goals, but it also created large unintended negative side effects. In a way, it was too successful."

Persuasive design is a methodology that focuses on influencing human behavior through a product or service's characteristics.[3] Many of today's digital methodologies were honed and taught by B.J. Fogg, a behavior scientist who is the founder and director of the Stanford Behavior Design Lab. He's also been called the millionaire maker as his work has inspired many of his students to create some of the world's addictive, and therefore more lucrative apps, games, and networks.[4] Defenders of these approaches state that they can also have positive effects on behavior, such as training people to take medicine regularly, develop weight loss habits, or learn new skills or subjects. However, it seems that harm is potentially outweighing good. In April 2018, 50 psychologists signed a letter to the American Psychological Association accusing psychologists working at tech companies of using persuasive design and to ask the APA to take an ethical stance on behalf of children.[5]

Developers knowingly use persuasive casino tricks and many exploitive design techniques that are directly linked to addiction in the games, networks, apps, and devices we use. These hidden "manipulation techniques" are used to hold our attention so it can be monetized.[6]

©rawpixel

To Influence behavioral change, you need motivation, ability, and triggers. For example, in social media, motivation can come in the form of people's need for attention, engagement, and social connection or on the other side, as the fear of missing out, or FOMO. Triggers include likes, comments, and connection requests. Research has shown that these triggers release delightful hits of chemical stimulants in our brains, such as oxytocin, serotonin, dopamine, and endorphins.

Awaken

Did you know slot machines make more money in the United States than baseball, movies, and theme parks combined? According to NYU professor Natasha Dow Schull, author

of *Addiction by Design*, slot machines are designed to addict. In her research, she found that people get "problematically involved" with slot machines three to four times faster than other forms of gambling.[7]

Slot machines are so addictive because they employ another psychological technique for enrapturing us, called *intermittent variable rewards*.[8] When you pull a lever, you hope to win a prize or reward. This is an intermittent action linked to a variable reward. The variable here is that you may win or, most likely, you may not win. The designer's goal is to keep you playing that machine in the hopes that you're going to win.

Former Google engineer Tristan Harris explains, "You pull a lever and immediately receive either an enticing reward (a match, a prize!) or nothing. Addictiveness is maximized when the rate of reward is most variable."[9] Software designers have incorporated this trick into all sorts of their products.

When you open your favorite app, check your email, and endlessly scroll or swipe, you're subconsciously trying to

Chapter 2

"win" something. But ask yourself, what exactly are you trying to win?

The manipulation is more obvious in the design of video games, which employ this as well as other addictive tactics. They offer all sorts of overt prizes for navigating their gauntlet of obstacles, but the real prize driving addiction to them is self-esteem. Richard Freed is a child and adolescent psychologist and the author of *Wired Child: Reclaiming Childhood in a Digital Age*.[10] He's discovered that video games are so addictive for boys because they have a particularly strong developmental drive to rack up accomplishments. All of the hidden cash boxes and points rewards they get, he explains, are designed "to make them feel like they are mastering something." The irony being that, as he says, this leads to "bad [gaming] habits and statistically poor academic performance."[11]

Another psychological hijack is *social reciprocity*. If someone pays you a compliment, for example, you feel the need to return the compliment. Or, if you ask for a favor, at some point, you will return that favor. If someone says, "Thank you," you feel compelled to respond with, "You're welcome." This can play out in digital life, as well. If you send an email, it's discourteous if the recipient doesn't reply right away. If you follow someone online, it's disrespectful (and even hurtful) if they don't follow you back.

> When you open your favorite app, check your email, and endlessly scroll or swipe, you're subconsciously trying to "win" something.

Awaken

©Sebastiaan Stam

This is why networks, for example, notify you when someone tags you in a post or lets you know when someone "read" your message. Or, when you send a message, you can see the wavering dots when someone is replying to you. And in some apps, you can see how long it's been since you've interacted with someone. You feel anticipation and pressure to stay engaged, to respond, to check back, to interact.

The anticipation of the experience is sometimes more powerful (and dangerous) than the experience itself. These engagement tricks or hacks are driving more usage than enjoyment. All the while, your attention is for sale. This is presumably why Bill Gates and Steve Jobs raised their kids tech-free.[12]

The technology companies have been engaged in a form of psychological warfare, competing in every way they can think of for our attention by exploiting our minds' weaknesses. It's only getting more competitive and, as a result, more dangerous. Ramsay Brown, the COO of start-up Dopamine Tech, admitted in an interview that his team uses artificial intelligence and neuroscience to make you even more addicted to your phone.[13]

"We use AI and neuroscience to increase your usage . . . make apps more persuasive . . . it's not an accident. It's a conscious design decision. We're designing minds. *The biggest tech companies in the world are always trying to figure out how to juice people.*"

In 2017 and 2018, the proverbial you-know-what hit the fan about all of this manipulation. Suddenly, all of technology's secrets were surfacing, their impact brought into greater focus by global events that demonstrated the darkest side of digital media.

© theverge.com © thenextweb.com

Awaken

"Former Facebook exec says social media is ripping apart society; No civil discourse, no cooperation; misinformation, mistruth."[14]

Sean Parker on Facebook: 'God only knows what it's doing to our children's brains'; Parker says he's become a 'conscientious objector' on social media"[15]

"Apple CEO becomes latest tech bigwig to warn of social media's dangers"[16]

At a conference in New York that promoted the importance of design ethics in digital technology, Tristan Harris said that a team of engineers at the company were controlling the minds of two billion users. "We have the power of gods without the wisdom, prudence and compassion of gods," he said. "It's a race to the bottom of the brain stem . . . getting people's attention at all costs."[17]

The Costs Are Great

Experts recommend spending 25 minutes to two hours working on a project at a time. If you're spending less than 25 minutes on an important or challenging task, then you're killing concentration and deflating your ability to warm up your brain before you quit. Your brain typically takes 23 minutes and 15 seconds to return to work following a distraction.[18]

I recently spent a year studying the effect of disruptive consumer technologies on our wellness and capacity for personal growth. I was hired by a global luxury beauty brand to specifically research the impact of consumer relationships with tech to understand its impact on interpretations of beauty, self-esteem, and happiness. Was a digital culture that encouraged teens to constantly take selfies eroding their confidence and making them obsess over achieving an unreachable standard of beauty? I interviewed women from the ages of 13 to 61, and my life was forever changed.

I was deeply concerned—horrified, actually—about the findings. While the research findings are confidential, I can say that women of all ages are measuring themselves by an impossible standard of beauty, with little or zero education, parenting, professional, or medical help to repair the destructive impact.

> Experts recommend spending 25 minutes to 2 hours working on a project at a time. If you're spending less . . . then you're killing concentration.

Awaken

Social media has also been linked to increased suicide by teens. For instance, research has found that an eighth-grader's risk for depression jumps 27% when he or she frequently uses social media, and depression is a leading indicator for suicide.[19] In fact, teen suicide now eclipses homicide rates in the United States, and smartphones and social media are the suspected culprits.[20]

Some of the strongest findings about ill-effects concern our constant switching between apps and real-world tasks, or what researchers call *rapid toggling* between tasks. In fact, we're not really multitasking as much as we're task-switching. Essentially, we are attempting to interact and progress while interchanging attention and context across devices and applications.

In her eye-opening TED Talk, Manoush Zomorodi, journalist and author of *Bored and Brilliant: How Spacing Out Can Unlock Your Most Productive and Creative Self,* shared a conversation with neurologist Dr. Daniel Levitin who said the following about switching between distractions.

"Every time you shift, you shift your attention, from one thing to another, the brain has to engage a neurochemical switch, that uses up nutrients in the brain to accomplish that. So, if you're attempting to multitask . . . doing four or five things at once, you're not actually doing four or five things at once, because the brain doesn't work that way. Instead, you're rapidly shifting from one thing to the next. Depleting neural resources as you go. And, we have a limited supply of that stuff."[21]

©Lilly Rum

We think we can multitask because it's normal. It's
what we do every day—text and walk, Snap/Insta and
drive, email and surf while in meetings, check our
phones while reading and studying. But with all this
multitasking, are we actually learning how to work
more efficiently? Well, science says *no*. While we
may believe we are capable of doing so, there are real
cognitive and opportunity costs attached to *alt-tab*-
ing between efforts. According to Guy Winch, PhD,
author of *Emotional First Aid: Practical Strategies for
Treating Failure, Rejection, Guilt and Other Everyday
Psychological Injuries,* "When it comes to attention and
productivity, our brains have a finite amount."[22] Doing so
many tasks at once leaves us with insufficient attentional
energy to do any of them really well.

Awaken

The corrosive effects of multitasking include:

Wastes time, attention, and energy[23]—While you may manage to produce some output, productivity, engagement, and value are usually compromised. As the late Clifford Nass at Stanford University demonstrated in his research, people who multitask do not pay attention, memorize, or manage their tasks as well as individuals who focus on one thing at a time.

Attacks output quality—Think you're great at multitasking? Bravo! Reports show that working on two or more projects simultaneously takes longer than if you worked on each one individually. Experts estimate that you suffer a 40% loss in productivity when you multitask. If you're not aiming for quality, you may work through multiple tasks, and do so quickly, but you actually create less and usually the value of your output suffers. You end up operating at a much more superficial level. Every time you take yourself out of the zone, it takes exponential time to get back into it before you can work at critical levels. Some trudge through it (that's me) and others become satisfied with average or substandard performance.

Makes you mistake prone—From typos to unexplained lapses in logic, random errors appear in everything you produce, because you're overwhelming the frontal cortex and not giving yourself enough depth and space for critical thinking.

Hinders intellectual and affective processes—One of the side effects of multitasking is skim reading. When the reading brain skims texts, "we don't have time to grasp complexity, to understand another's feelings or to perceive beauty," according to Maryanne Wolf of UCLA.[24] By compromising our intellectual and affective processes, we impair our internalized knowledge, our comprehension and ability to grasp complexity, analogical reasoning and inference, perspective-taking, empathy, and critical analysis. UCLA psychologist Patricia Greenfield warns that less attention and time will be allocated to slower, time-demanding, deep reading processes.[25] Multitasking "prevents people from getting a deeper understanding of information," Greenfield said.

Causes stress—When you are switching between tasks, you place yourself in a mode of *high alert* or *on the edge*. Your true creativity is not kindled. Instead, your heart rate is up, and you produce the stress hormone cortisol.[26] The pressure you feel triggers anxiety during and in-between tasks. Over time, performance in this mode can provoke chronic stress, self-esteem issues, and even depression.

Awaken

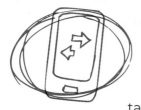

Makes you miss out on life—If you're multitasking, you're missing out on many things on many fronts. Something as simple as walking and talking/texting/messaging makes you miss the beauty of your surroundings. Taking pictures or shooting videos might capture the images around you, but this doesn't necessarily allow your experiences to reverberate emotionally inside you. This *inattentional blindness* prevents your brain from processing experiences that inspire thinking and creativity. Furthermore, if it takes longer for you to complete tasks, you miss out on time for fun.

Affects your memory—Have you ever lost your train of thought or a common word in the middle of a story? Have you ever stood still and asked yourself, "What was I about to do?" Switching between tasks disrupts short-term memory.[27] A 2016[28] study found that multitaskers exhibit weakness in working memory (the ability to store relevant information while working on a task) and long-term memory (the ability to store and recall information over longer periods of time). Other studies show that when you are interrupted, or if you interrupt yourself, you miss or forget details in the moment and as you continue your work.[29]

Extinguishes creativity—Just like your laptop or tablet uses RAM (random access memory) to give you rapid working ability in your open tabs/

windows, human multitasking uses working memory or temporary brain storage. The University of Illinois at Chicago found that jumping between activities exhausts this finite memory and leaves little or no energy for creativity. You're literally spent. More so, you're never truly in the moment. You don't give yourself the creative freedom to explore possibilities and build on them. *Attention residue* often limits you from starting with a blank canvas. Many times, you're thinking of another task while working on the one in front of you.

Lowers IQ—Not only does multitasking slow you down; it lowers your IQ, according to research conducted by the University of London.[30] As I referenced before, during cognitive tasks, research participants who multitask experienced declines in IQ scores that were similar to the effects of staying up all night or smoking marijuana. In fact, the scores of multitasking men dropped to the average range of an 8-year-old child.

Leads to increased distractibility— You've been there many times. You're working on something, you switch to check your streams, you see a link, you click it, and then 30 minutes later, you're wondering what just happened to the last half hour. You fell into online rabbit holes. Researchers have found that multitaskers exhibit increased behavioral distractibility.[31] Your addiction deepens.[32]

Hurts your relationships—At the most basic level, whether you're with loved ones, friends, colleagues, managers, teachers, and so on, if you break moments of engagement to mindlessly multitask, your actions, maybe not your words, say, "I'm only partially in this moment right now with you." It's often referred to as *technoference*, and it signifies to the people you're with physically that they aren't your priority.[33] Even if you're not looking at devices, because you're so wired to multitask, your mind is unfocused, flying off in a dozen different directions. Exclusive attention, listening, giving yourself, and investing these currencies into a relationship define the relationship. It's hard to do, which is why it's so special.

Saps your energy—The cognitive costs are just one of the many assets you'll spend by multitasking. There are biological and emotional costs, as well. You're expending exorbitant energy, exhausting the oxygenated glucose in your brain.[34] You're running down the fuel needed to focus.

Can be dangerous—The more you multitask, the more it becomes second nature. Read this. It becomes almost like breathing. You don't think about its dangers, which is why so many people use their phones while driving. Or if you're one of the more responsible folks, you wait until stoplights to check your phone. You're driving or riding or moving under the influence. Even walking is dangerous. One study in New York

City found that 20% of teenagers struck in crosswalks were on their devices. Ironically, they're often hit by *smartphone zombie drivers*.[35] Just Google the number of accidents caused by zombie smartphone use. Go to YouTube and watch videos. Watch how quickly you get disgusted.

 **May damage your brain**—Researchers from the University of Sussex used MRI scans to compare the brains of multitaskers and normal people.[36] They discovered that multitaskers had less brain density in gray matter, specifically the anterior cingulate cortex.[37] I had to look that up. It's the area of the brain responsible for empathy and also cognitive and emotional control. Over- or underreact much? In all seriousness, while IQ is critical to success, EQ (emotional intelligence) is also important. For example, TalentSmart tested more than one million employees and found that 90% of top performers have high EQ scores. Multitasking is shown to lower IQ and if we read the MRI scans correctly, the same can be true for EQ.

©Eric Ward

We Are Culpable in Our Addiction

The gut-punching truth is that distraction has become one of our values. We actually welcome and enjoy it. The ability to manage distraction has even emerged as a new competency, according to New Yorker editor Joshua Rothman, and it's one that we, perhaps subconsciously, feel proud of.[38]

> Distractions are largely welcome because they can temporarily save us from contending with the challenge of a difficult task . . . loneliness, fear, self-doubt, self-loathing, and insecurity.

What is the basis of our willingness to be distracted? Often, the allure of distractions is a by-product of our desire to avoid contending with problems in our lives, which we may not even have yet recognized.

Blaise Pascal, French mathematician, physicist, inventor, writer, and source of so many quotes we've read and shared in our lives, astutely observed, "All men's miseries derive from not being able to sit in a quiet room alone."[39] The irony is that we convince ourselves that such alone time would force us to focus on problems we're facing, which would cause us more pain.

Some experts believe that distractions are largely welcome because they can temporarily save us from contending with the challenge of a difficult task, or personal matters such as loneliness, fear, anxiety, self-doubt, self-loathing, and insecurity.[40] There's also the very real problem that many of us do not enjoy the work we're doing.

~~Distractions are an escape.~~

Brandon Crawford, coauthor of *The World Beyond Your Head: Becoming an Individual in an Age of Distraction*, has another explanation for the appeal.[41] He believes that at the heart of this succumbing to distraction is autonomy run amok. "We've taken things too far; we're now addicted to liberation," he asserts. In his view, anything we have to do in any situation is a kind of prison. So, giving in to distraction becomes a way of asserting control. We give ourselves an escape to exert our autonomy, generating a false, short-lived sense of freedom.

It's not easy to see that we're doing this. I certainly didn't understand what was happening to me—how addicted I'd become to distraction. Without that knowledge, I couldn't learn how to heal. I couldn't rediscover my creativity and intentionally regain happiness if I didn't believe or feel they were lost in the first place.

It's easier to offer advice than it is to digest it, and it's easier to absorb it than it is to act on it and bring change to our lives. To admit problems in the way we're living causes discomfort, even pain, which automatically activates our defenses to save us from those difficulties. In a cruel twist of logic, our efforts to save ourselves often lead us into denial. All of our technological distractions have made that easier for us because they are designed to seem so useful and nurturing. What could be wrong with sharing our photos with friends? News alerts might inform us of something we really need to know. What if there's an accident on our normal route to work? Certainly, we should leave our phones on at all times if

Awaken

we've got kids in school. What if we're not there to get a text that a child is sick? And on and on and on.

When I bit the bullet and admitted I had a problem, I could begin to unravel what lay beneath all of my obsessive multitasking and unacknowledged tech addictions, and I began to see how my work, and my relationships, were suffering. That was when I devoted myself to learning how to heal. *Awareness is awakening.*

Your own distraction probably snuck up on you, too, and perhaps you believe that you're getting by just fine. Maybe you're still keeping up with your work and nurturing your relationships pretty well. My advice is don't let the problem fester until you run into a crisis like I did. Think of it this way:

Let's say you have a car that has been showing annoying signs of issues over the last year. Sometimes the car suddenly stops running for no apparent reason when you pull up to a light, or before you've finished pulling into a parking space. "That's weird," you think, but a quick key turn or button push and the car starts right back up. So, you keep driving it. You're too busy to take it in for repair. You always have some place to be and this

is really just a nuisance; it's a lower priority than everything else on your packed agenda.

But now, let's say that the car starts stalling almost every time you come to a stop.

Let's also say that you're on your way to the most important event of your life. The car just keeps shutting down, at every light, every stop sign. You're overwhelmed with helplessness. You have to get to this event! You could kick yourself for not getting the car fixed.

We have to prioritize taking care of our bodies and minds; otherwise they're at some point going to fail us, and we can't know what marvelous life experiences we'll start missing out on.

Awaken

We Can Take Our Attention Back

Every day when you wake up without a new, intentional mindset and resolve to change your trajectory toward a more positive vision and more productive behavior, you are, by default, beginning your day just as you did yesterday and the day before that. You are caught in a legacy trap, a routine of current behaviors and beliefs that govern your day and life ahead. You can never truly move forward without a conscious effort. You can only optimize the paradigm you're in now. Each day we further hardwire that cyclical programming. We can either become aware of our behaviors and how they're affecting us, or we can continue with the status quo.

Yes, our ability to think deeply and create are victims of the manipulations of digital capitalism. But you are now mindful of how your mind is being attacked and manipulated. You stand at a crossroads. What you do from this moment on is your choice. You can transform your FOMO from *fear of missing out* to *finally over missing out*. Awareness is where the journey toward a healthier, mindful, and fantastically creative life begins.

You were not put on this planet to validate your existence through the false validation of strangers. You are more important, able, and beautiful beyond any number of likes, comments, or followers can attest. You can find a new path by living your life as if no one is watching.

©Stefan Cosma

REFOCUS

Reclaim Your
Attention:
Simple
First
Steps

> "Who you are, what you think, feel, and do,
> what you love—is the sum of what you focus on"
> – Winifred Gallagher

Now that we've realized we have a major problem, the next step in lifescaling is to learn how to concentrate again by establishing positive and productive daily routines.

Georgetown professor Cal Newport observed, "High-quality work produced is a function of two things—the amount of time you spend on the work and the intensity of your focus during this time."[1] Increasing your focus will ignite your creativity and help you get more done in less time, while also amplifying the quality of work.

There is no shortage of resources available to help you focus as you launch into your creative ventures. Trust me; I looked everywhere, talked to everyone, and read all that I could. Would-be resource centers are overflowing with platitudes that offer shallow tips, as well as attention-grabbing listicles of generic recommendations masquerading as life-changing prescriptions. My search was exhausting, and I found trying to sort through the glut of advice enormously frustrating. So, here I'll provide a few simple solutions for breaking the bad habits of disruption that I've found hugely helpful.

> "High-quality work produced is a function of two things—the amount of time you spend on the work and the intensity of your focus during this time."

But first, let me address a harmful myth about focus that's gained widespread currency.

Did you know that you have the attention span of a goldfish? Actually, a goldfish holds a one second advantage over you, according to a research report. Apparently, you (and I) can only concentrate for eight whole consecutive seconds, whereas a goldfish can focus for a whopping nine seconds.[2] And what's especially frightening is how rapidly our attention span has been eroding. When it was measured in 2008, it was twelve seconds. So, we've lost four seconds in five years! What will we be down to in another five?

Do not believe this.

When I dug into the basis of this claim, I discovered that the so-called study that generated this meme is a prime example of what I call *short attention span theater.*

@Kilyan Sockalingum

Details about the research process were scarce at best. Here's what we do know. The report was sponsored by the advertising office of Microsoft Canada. The authors are not named, and the source of the eight second figure is a website called Statistic Brain, which offers zero sources of its own about the information it provides. Dig deeper, and not only does something smell fishy; the whole thing is bait. I couldn't actually find any real research that pinpoints the exact attention span of goldfish.

> We haven't lost our ability to focus at all. We just need to reclaim it. We can unlearn disruptive behaviors, learn new skills, and build new routines that help us chart the new course of lifescaling.

Think about it. When you binge-watch your favorite show, are you only able to watch it in eight-second bursts? How absurd! Similarly, I'll bet a goldfish could focus on eating for longer than nine seconds if it had to.

Let me propose an alternative outlook. We haven't lost our ability to focus at all. We just need to reclaim it. We can unlearn disruptive behaviors, learn new skills, and build new routines that help us chart the new course of lifescaling.

Refocus

Practicing a set of simple techniques will free up our energy and intention to help us take the next steps on the journey. We're not trying to make one big dive into sustained concentration, like going cold turkey. We'll get to building up our deep focus later. For now, it's best to take incremental and relatively painless steps. I call this *attention hacking.* [3]

@Dan Gold

Remember the story of the car that breaks down? Attention hacks are like quick fixes to get your car going. Like aid from a helpful fellow motorist who sees you in distress and pulls up and says, "Hey, I can fix that." You pop the hood and this kind person adjusts a few things that help your car idle at a higher RPM. Now, you can make it to your event! Is your car really fixed? No. But, you *will* get to the event. And, following the event, you can take your car into the shop to fix the core problem that was causing the breakdowns in the first place.

Attention hacks provide immediate relief that frees up our minds to begin the more substantial work of actually curing our distraction. They're small fixes to get you moving forward.

These are all hacks I've experimented with while researching and writing this book. They don't demand radical behavioral shifts and can produce incredible results. There is no single hack sufficient to reclaim your powers of focus, but in combination these techniques can get you solidly on a path to repair. Before long, you'll be moving forward at an accelerated pace, and I'll bet you'll even start coming up with some of your own hacks. You will relish the relief hacks bring.

Attention hacks provide immediate relief that frees up our minds to begin the more substantial work of actually curing our distraction.

Procrastinate Procrastination

For the first year of trying to write my proposal for what I hoped would be my next book (but that thankfully led to this book), I built up so much anxiety before each scheduled work session that I would do anything else besides write. Clean the house. Organize the garage. Hell, I'd even take out the garbage.

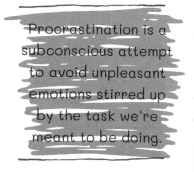

Procrastination is a
subconscious attempt to avoid
unpleasant emotions stirred
up by the task we're meant
to be doing. Whether it's fear,
worry, anxiety, shame, anger,
panic, or even FOMO, avoidance
behaviors give us a momentary
reprieve. The irony is, though, that procrastination ultimately intensifies the very negative emotions we're trying to evade, because it leads to actual urgency to complete a task.

@Andrik Langfield

Chapter 3

After deep self-reflection as a result of embracing the idea and need for this book, I realized that the negative emotions I was trying to circumvent were shame and self-doubt. Somewhere along the way, I lost the joy of creation. I was creating perfunctorily and tackling creative projects transactionally. I was cranking out work as fast as I could and moving right on to the next project. In the process, I wasn't dancing with imagination. I wasn't inspired. Creation had become a chore. Happiness wasn't even a memory. I had forgotten about the relationship between achievement and ecstasy. I didn't celebrate my moments, and this led to drudgery.

At the end of every day, rather than feeling great about the work I'd accomplished, as I used to, I felt no sense of fulfillment or pride in the work. Over time, as I kept trudging through projects, I actually felt progressively worse about myself, increasingly doubting my creativity and performance. I was caught in a vicious cycle of self-defeat. I even began questioning whether I wanted to maintain the level of success I'd achieved. I was unwittingly practicing self-sabotage. What's more, I didn't actually realize the extent to which I was underperforming.

Thankfully my research into procrastination showed the way out. We can choose to succumb to the waves of difficult emotions that lead us to procrastinate, or we can plant our feet, brace ourselves, and let each wave pass.

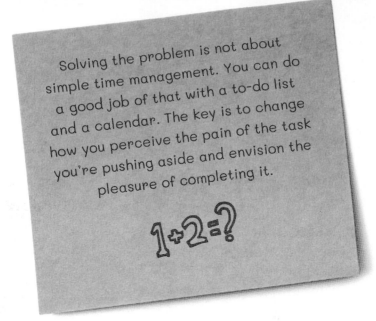

Solving the problem is not about simple time management. You can do a good job of that with a to-do list and a calendar. The key is to change how you perceive the pain of the task you're pushing aside and envision the pleasure of completing it.

1+2=?

Solving the problem is not about simple time management. You can do a good job of that with a to-do list and a calendar. The key is to change how you perceive the pain of the task you're pushing aside and envision the pleasure of completing it. A great way to do this is with mental projection.[3]

Instead of focusing on the negative attributes of a pending project, visualize the tangible benefits and the feelings that will result from the timely and exceptional delivery of your project. Take a little time to do that right now with something you've been putting off. What message of appreciation might you receive for doing it? What joy will you feel in the accomplishment? Also visualize the outcome you don't want to happen. Now, discipline yourself to sit with the difficult feelings that arise in response to this exercise for a few minutes, and then return to envisioning achievement.

Chapter 3

@Clark Tibbs

Legendary boxer and showman Muhammad Ali dreaded training. He once famously said,[4] "I hated every minute of training, but I said, 'Don't quit. Suffer now and live the rest of your life as a champion.'"

If you can't visualize it, you can't achieve it. If you can't appreciate it, you can't learn and build upon those learnings to celebrate accomplishments and progress. We are our own thieves of happiness. We rob ourselves of the little moments that are actually transports of contentment now and in the long-term.

Refocus

Good Morning, Brain.

Even making a dent in your next creative project is enough to flush negativity out of your mind, body, and soul. A great way to get going is to prioritize what's important at the beginning of your day.

For years, I started my morning with emails and coffee and then stacked meetings and calls following, so that I could focus on important projects for the rest of the day. By the time I was ready to think critically and wanted to draw on my creativity for deeper projects, I was already low on initiative, imagination, and drive.  I couldn't dive beyond the shallows without incredible effort. By the end of the evening, when I would return to my desk after dinner and tucking in my girls for the night, I would sit in front of my screen, desperately trying to activate my mind. I found myself constantly chasing the very distractions I was intent on avoiding! I told myself that doing so might just be the spark of creativity I needed. Maybe a great article would ignite my passion, or a marvelous video would pump me up.

I was expending precious creative fuel I desperately needed, and I accomplished very little while sacrificing valuable time I should have been using to relax and restore. I would have to abandon lots of mediocre output and write-off the wasted time and energy so as to not affect my overall work quality and professional reputation.

Had I only been aware of how much more productive my brain could be right after a good night of some quality downtime and good sleep, who knows what I could have accomplished.

> Our body replenishes our creative juices to begin each day with our full potential.

Prioritizing your day with the most important projects at the beginning gives you a fresh start with a reset brain that has released its mental exhaust. Research shows that our brains are much sharper in the morning. In fact, I learned that our brains are actually bigger,[5] literally, in the morning. The Montreal Neurological Institute analyzed almost 10,000 MRI scans and found that the brain shrinks over the course of the day only to return to its full size the next morning.[6] The team compared the brain to a sponge, which begins fully hydrated in the morning due to the redistribution of fluids during sleep. Our body replenishes our creative juices to begin each day with our full potential.

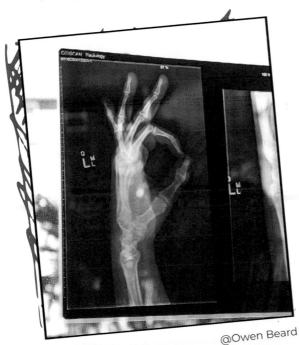

@Owen Beard

Now maybe you're one of those people who are night owls, who thrive on the solitude of late evenings and find that's your most creative, productive part of the day. Research in the field of chronobiology has validated that some people have different circadian rhythms, and that it's best not to fight our natural rhythms.[7] But you still need to make sure you're getting a good amount of sleep. With that condition, adjusting your schedule to your biology is just fine; the key point is that you need to plug into your brain when it is at its prime. And for most of us, that's in the morning.

So, I suggest for most of you that you schedule first thing in the morning[5] for deeper projects and allocate blocks later in the day to less demanding work like checking emails and answering the ones that just need a quick reply, doing your filing, and having one-on-one meetings with your staff. The evening before, decide what your next day looks like and stick to the plan. Do not cancel or reschedule these appointments with creativity. This is your time. This is "the present you" making time for a "future you." And the importance of this part cannot be overstated—go through that list of accomplishments each day, and smile. Cross things off your list and savor your productivity.

Single-task as a matter of ritual

This is easier said than done. I get it. But hopefully, the litany of harmful effects from multitasking in the previous chapter will convince you to try. Once you are working on your scheduled important morning task, work on it with rigorously minimized distractions.

Turn off notifications in important moments.

Did you know that we have two separate attention networks? There's a conscious system that allows us to focus on tasks at hand. Then there is an unconscious network, and it is very vulnerable to distraction.[8] It shifts focus toward whatever external or internal signals our senses pick up in a moment.[9] Even though your conscious mind may be 100% focused on whatever's important, your unconscious attention network never shuts down. This is a key reason that all of our tech distractions are so hard to ignore.

Keep this in mind as you begin work each morning: It's estimated that mobile phone users receive upwards of 200 notifications per day.[10] That's not including the daily real-world distractions they receive within the same period. The struggle with notifications is that they cause information overload in compounding microdoses.

Notifications are a self-defeating temptation meant to fool you into believing that you only matter when people are reacting to or reaching out to you. They are designed to create an intoxicating feedback loop of rewards from internal stimulants that make us feel good because we're being noticed, and people want our attention.

Refocus

They are horribly damaging to your productivity. Research shows that when you switch away from your primary task to check email, respond to a text, check your social media status, or whatever, you add to the total time it takes to complete your main project by an average of 25%.[11]

So, turn off all notifications on your system. Do it. Go on Do Not Disturb or Airplane mode on your smartphone. Also, clean up your desktop and close unnecessary windows, browser tabs, and apps.

©Nito

Take a different kind of break

Essential to revitalizing focus as you move through the day is taking strategically timed breaks. Whether you work for 25 minutes and take a five-minute break, or you push through one-hour intervals and take a 15-minute break, try using breaks to do something you wouldn't normally do. Instead of opening email, checking notifications, or surfing the web, do something personally rewarding.

For instance, stand up, close your eyes, and stretch. Bend over and try to touch your toes and hold the position for 20 seconds. Try to do as many pushups as you can. (I recently joined the 100-pushups-a-day club!) Go for a quick walk. Deliver a hug to someone close by. Call someone special and tell them you love them. Convey a compliment to someone who deserves it. Recall a joyful event and smile. Whatever it is, do something that makes you feel good before you get back to your masterpiece.

Work in sprints

If I can be transparent with you, at the beginning, I couldn't get past six minutes without catching myself impulsively jumping to other tabs, reaching for a device or getting up for some reason, like to grab yet another coffee, do some cleaning, or organize my closet. I'd realize that I was mindlessly shuffling through the stuff on my desk, or lost in daydreaming.

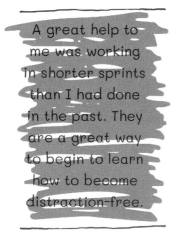

A great help to me was working in shorter sprints than I had done in the past. They are a great way to begin to learn how to become distraction-free. Even this short sprint approach is not without its challenges, however. It may sound easy, but as you'll experience, focusing for 25 distraction-free minutes or more demonstrates exactly why we're going through this exercise. I found one method for sticking with my sprints especially helpful.

It's called the Pomodoro Technique. Inspired by the Pomodoro kitchen timer, this time management method was developed by Francesco Cirillo[12] in the late 1980s. It uses the timer, or in my case a mobile phone and desktop app, to break down workflows into approachable 25-minute sprints, separated by five-minute breaks.

©Sergey Vasutin

Here's how the process works:

- Choose a task to be accomplished.

- Set the Pomodoro to 25 minutes.

- Work on the task until the Pomodoro rings, then put a check on your sheet of paper (or the app) related to the project.

- Take a five-minute break.

- After every four Pomodoros, take a longer break (usually between 15–30 minutes).

Refocus

While 25 minutes might not seem like a long time, or perhaps it does (it did for me!), think of it as a block of output. And as with building blocks, they stack up fast, and each one will contribute vitally to completion.

Over time you can carve out longer time periods for sprints. I'm now working toward flows of focusing for 40 minutes and then taking 20-minute breaks. Some productivity experts have recommended 52-minute sprints and 17-minute breaks, which will be my next step.

The 52-minute increment comes from a study[13] published by DeskTime, a company that develops a popular time-tracking app, in which the researchers found that the app's most productive 10 percent of users take breaks after working intently for close to one hour. Here's how they described their findings:

> The reason the most productive 10% of our users are able to get the most done during the comparatively short periods of working time is that their working times are treated as sprints. They make the most of those 52 minutes by working with intense purpose, but then rest up to be ready for the next burst. During the 52 minutes of work, you're dedicated to accomplishing tasks, getting things done, and making progress. Whereas, during the 17 minutes of break, you're completely removed from the work you're doing—you're entirely resting, not peeking at your email every five minutes or just "quickly checking Facebook."

The longest increment recommended for sprints is 90 minutes, which is inspired by the research of Nathaniel Kleitman. He identified what he calls the "basic rest–activity cycle."[14] In his work, Kleitman found that our brains work in 90-minute rest–activity cycles as we traverse the five stages of sleep—from alertness to deep sleep. His studies also observed that our bodies follow a similar 90-minute rhythm when we're awake. When it comes to productivity, he proposed that we are at our peak at the top of a 90-minute cycle and that our productivity declines from there until we reset the clock.

As we go through the rest of the book together, try to keep expanding your work blocks from 25 minutes to 40 or 52 minutes, and if you want to try it, go on ahead to 90 minutes. I know you will be thrilled with how you're building discipline and forming a whole new habit.

To begin, right now:

1. Schedule time for one project tomorrow morning.

2. Block out 25 minutes on your calendar.

3. Tomorrow morning, hang the Do Not Disturb sign physically and digitally.

4. Turn off notifications.

5. Turn off your phone.

6. Turn off email.

7. Close all those tabs—you know what I'm talking about.

8. Resist temptation to indulge in any diversion, regardless of how quick or seemingly harmless.

9. Put on your headphones.

10. Have refreshments at the ready.

11. Use the restroom.

12. Start the clock, and

Focus.

Life Is Less Alive
without Creativity

> "Every child is an artist. The problem is how
> to remain an artist once we grow up."
> – Pablo Picasso

The one thing we all share, just like the moon, the stars, and the sun, is that we were all artists when we were young.

Creativity isn't just for geniuses, the elite, the weirdos, or the gifted. The pursuit or practice of creativity, even if your output is nothing like that of Leonardo da Vinci, benefits you and those around you.

Why?

Creativity engages the mind by challenging us. It encourages critical thinking and allows us to more easily absorb knowledge,[1] solve problems,[2] see new opportunities, innovate, and invent.

© John Baker

Chapter 4

Creativity stops time whereas distractions waste time and expedite its passing. If you've ever experienced deep work or creative flows, you'll attest that time has stopped. Not only does creativity enhance quality and productivity; you feel self-assured and more capable because of it.

Creativity opens us to empathy, allowing us to better connect with ourselves and others. It opens both our minds and our hearts, revealing untapped resources to see and do things differently.

Creativity stimulates reflection, enhancing our self-awareness and our connection to our authentic aspirations. It calls on us to switch out of mindless consumption of all the output of others—all those tweets and posts and streaming cat videos—and focus on what *we* can offer.

Creativity helps us build self-confidence by allowing us to create work that delights others and to discover hidden talents.

Creativity gives a voice to parts of ourselves we didn't know existed and helps us communicate through alternative, personal, and powerful forms of self-expression.[3]

We grow and learn because of creativity. We open our minds. And our acts of creation pull us toward meditative states, which sharpens intuition and creativity itself while also reducing stress and anxiety.

Believe

Without creativity, we would dwell in comfort zones, mediocrity, and complacency. Without creativity, there would be no innovation. Creativity pushes us to take risks,[4] which can open new doors. And even though the popular narrative is that taking risks can lead to judgment by our peers and consequences of deviating from the norm and potential failures, it can also lead to extraordinary outcomes that would otherwise not have been possible.

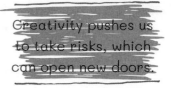

Creativity pushes us to take risks, which can open new doors.

Creative thinkers understand and appreciate the success in failure. They accept that missteps are essential on the way to new frontiers. As Scott Adams, creator of Dilbert, once said about creativity and failure, "Creativity is allowing yourself to make mistakes. Art is knowing which ones to keep."[5]

We all have a deep well of creativity, but for so many of us, we've lost the sense of its depths within us.

George Bernard Shaw once observed, "Youth is wasted on the young." It could also be said that youth is taken from them.

To riff on the Pink Floyd song "Remember When You Were Young," you once shone like the sun, radiating creative joy.[6] But as the years go on, the artist within each of us dims a bit more each day if we don't entertain our inspirations or passions.

Once upon a time, we freely let rip with our creativity. Our loved ones used to tell us how wonderful our little creations were. Our masterpieces hung on our school walls, at home on our refrigerators, and were the source of many family albums. For those who have children, we still celebrate and cherish the work of these little geniuses.

Art by Brian's daughter

We were dreamers. We used to build forts, conquer dragons, and have adventures in magical places. We used to be kings, queens, princes, and princesses. We were once heroes in our own worlds! I believe we still are.

What breaks my heart is that for most of us, at some point in life our creative spark is smothered. We *tell* children—not *ask* them—to tuck away their creativity and focus on the future. Okay kids, playtime is over. It's time to grow up, because at some point, we all have to. Society values production and there's no GDP for quality of life or artistry.

Believe

> We tell children—not ask them—to tuck away their creativity and focus on the future.

So, we part ways with the magic of youthful creativity. No more crayons. No more watercolors. No more instruments to play. No more clay and castles. No more construction paper or shoe boxes. We're done entertaining that side of our brains. Your creative spirit is no longer appreciated; we need you to learn how to *work*. You have to make a living after all. And to do so, we need you to follow the rules—the rules by which society defines success. The rules defined for us by the generations who've worked so hard to give us the blessings we have today. Well, at least that's what we're taught.

© Karl Fredrickson

A while ago, I read an unforgettable article that had a very special video attached to it. The headline read, "How Society Kills Your Creativity."[7] I stopped everything to read it and watch the video. Let me share with you the powerful paragraphs that struck me so deeply:

When it comes to our modern-day society, there is no doubt that we are being told how to live and what our lives are supposed to look like. When we are born we have our parents imposing their ideas and beliefs onto us about what is right and what is wrong and then from there we are usually enrolled into the public school system. Here is where a lot of our natural, inherent creative abilities unfortunately come to die.

In many cases, the school system doesn't celebrate gifts in the realm of art, music, poetry, etc. Rather, the more logical, analytical ways of knowledge are celebrated, such as math, science, and memorization. Sure, these are important gifts as well and they should be celebrated, but not all people fit into that mold. And then what happens to those gifts that are left untapped and never brought forward into our world for everyone to enjoy? Well, society wants us to believe that those gifts do not fit into our system and we can't make a living by utilizing them. What a conundrum.

Believe

The article's author, Kasim Khan, founder of Education Inspire Change (EIC), introduces the work of Madrid-based animators, Daniel Martinez Lara and Rafa Cano Mendez and their critically acclaimed short film *Alike*.[8] This profoundly moving, seven-minute short teaches us a heartfelt lesson of what happens to us when we ignore imagination, silence our creativity, and mute our talents. The film also portrays the flourishing that comes from setting our children, and ourselves, free from the creativity-sapping pressures of society and allowing our creative spirits to thrive by unleashing our imaginations and chasing artistic pursuits—even if just for fun. Imagine society if we all absorbed the lessons of this film.

Alike tells the story of a father and his young son and the daily routines by which they begin and end their days. Each morning, they get ready for school, both bright in their colors; the father is blueish, the son orangish. As they walk to school with glee, each enjoying the company of the other, you immediately notice that all the other characters, hunched and slogging their way to school and work, are a drab gray in color. So are the buildings and streets. As our two protagonists make their way to school, they pass a small park, full of color, where a man is playing a violin. He, too, is in color. I suppose you see where this is going.

The young boy stops, drops his backpack, and runs back to watch the performance, beginning to play along as though he too holds a violin, with a look of joy and wonder on his face. But they must move on. The father retrieves the backpack and with the son wavering left to right from the weight of the backpack, crammed with all the books he's got to be studying, they make their way to his school.

In a clever split scene, we watch the boy and his father both settle into their daily routine. The child is in class learning how to write his ABCs. The father is buried under a skyscraper of paperwork, removing one sheet from the towering pile at a time. He slowly begins to turn gray. And it breaks our heart.

At the same time, his son proudly displays his first attempt at drawing his ABCs, but he hasn't been working on them. Instead, he's been drawing a picture, to the best of his ability, of the man and his violin in the park. His teacher, none too pleased, hands the child another worksheet and instructs him to try again. His smile turns into a frown. But then he thinks, smiles, and tries again. This time, his alphabet is rich in creative

Believe

interpretations of each letter: A = a smiling person, B = a bee in the shape of the capital letter, C = a magnet, D is shaped like a sideways ladybug.

At the end of the day, the father, grayed out and exhausted, sees his son coming to meet him to walk home. The boy, seeing his father, immediately smiles, drops his backpack, and races toward him. They embrace in a hug that would make you believe they'd been apart for days. And as they hug, the father's color is quickly restored. But day in and day out, the father returns to his routines and his son is introduced to his own set of monotonous regimens.

As time goes on and the child is taught to conform, he slowly loses his orange color. He no longer restores his father's color with an embrace at the end of the day; instead he glumly hands over that day's assignment. But the son returns sometimes to the park to listen to the violinist, and some of his color is restored each time. He is managing to keep some spark alive.

Then one day, while in the office, the father, clearly disturbed at the growing distance in their relationship, stops his work to review his son's drawing of the violinist, which he keeps on his desk. The camera slowly zooms in on his face, the music slows, and we can almost see inside his mind that he suddenly realizes the dispiriting effects of imposing society's conventions, and his own conformity, upon his son without balancing it with opportunities for creative expression.

The next morning, as they are walking to school and work, the father holds up the son's drawing of the man and his violin in the park. Then, with a small head gesture and a gleam in his eyes, he suggests that they take a detour to the park. The little boy beams.

But as they approach, they see that the man and his violin are not there, and the child's smile fades. He drops his head, turns, and begins to trudge to school. But he realizes his father isn't walking with him, and looking back, he sees him standing in the park. The father gently sets down his briefcase, makes eye contact with his son, looks around as if wondering whether he should really do what he's contemplating, clenches and releases his fists a couple of times, breathes in, and then gracefully takes the stance of a violinist and begins to enthusiastically play air violin.

Several gray people stop to stare with beady black eyes, but the young boy is beaming again. Father and son regain their color. The boy leaps into his father's arms for a huge hug, as the background fades, and suddenly it's just father and son sharing a wondrous moment.

Just like the father in Alike, our inner big-eyed, anything-is-possible, artist and dreamer is still there inside of us Yours is there right now, just hoping to one day be free again.

For years, I've followed the work of David Kelley and Tom Kelley and have been fortunate enough to be part of an informal think tank where they, and many other brilliant minds, host quarterly dinners and talk about the state and future of innovation. David is the founder of the groundbreaking design firm IDEO, and Tom is a founder of the Hasso Platter Institute of Design at Stanford. They coauthored the bestselling *Creative Confidence, Unleashing the Creative Potential Within Us All.*

Too often, the Kelley brothers assert, companies and individuals assume that creativity and innovation are the domain of only the *creative types.*

It turns out that creativity isn't some rare gift to be enjoyed by the lucky few—it's a natural part of human thinking and behavior. In too many of us it gets blocked. But it can be unblocked. And unblocking that creative spark can have far-reaching implications for yourself, your organization, and your community.

Believe

David Kelley gave a great TED talk in which he focused on this theme.[9] Every TED speaker is supposed to leave the audience with a request about "how to change the world." Kelly's request was: "Don't divide the world into the creatives and the non-creatives, like it's some God-given thing. And, to have people realize that they're naturally creative ... that those people should let their ideas fly ... that you can do what you set out to do ... and that you can reach a place of creative confidence."

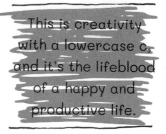

This is creativity with a lowercase c, and it's the lifeblood of a happy and productive life.

Being creative isn't as much a talent or gift as it is a choice. Yes, there are people who can create mind-blowing art, who are natural geniuses. That's Creativity with a *Big C.* But for every example of capital *C* creativity, there are multitudes of human beings with the power and ability to solve everyday problems and uncover new possibilities, even in the smallest of things or instances, as well as those who simply seek to be better in certain aspects of their life. This is creativity with a lowercase c, and it's the lifeblood of a happy and productive life.

Your Creativity Is of Great Value

Sir Ken Robinson, a British author, speaker, and international advisor on education in the arts, defines creativity as, in its very essence, *original ideas that have value.* By failing to nurture imagination and creativity in our youth, young adults, and adults alike (see what I did there?), we are robbing the world of that value. Meanwhile, in this time of great disruption, creativity, which fuels innovation, is dearly needed.

Robinson cautions, "We don't grow into creativity, we grow out of it. Or rather, we get educated out of it." [10]

"We don't grow into creativity, we grow out of it. Or rather, we get educated out of it."

Don't play an instrument; you'll never earn a living as a musician.

Don't paint, draw, or sculpt; you'll only sell your work enough to get by if you're lucky.

Don't learn to act or dance; you'll have to take on a menial job while you pursue work.

Do not believe in these soul-crushing rules; believe in the power of your creativity. You have distinctive creative gifts to offer. Everyone should believe they are special. I hope you believe you're special, because you are. Only you can make the unique contributions you have to offer. Do not underestimate how valuable they are.

Many highly talented, brilliant, creative people think they're not because the thing that they were good at in school wasn't valued or was actually stigmatized.

As Ken Robinson says, "Many highly talented, brilliant, creative people think they're not because the thing that they were good at in school wasn't valued or was actually stigmatized. I think we can't afford to go on that way." [11]

Believe

In his 2007 TED Talk, Robinson tells the incredible story of Gillian Lynne to illustrate this perspective.[12] She was a renowned British ballerina and choreographer, celebrated for the elegant dances she crafted for Andrew Lloyd Webber's *Phantom of the Opera* and the sinuous movements in *Cats*, one of the longest-running musicals on Broadway.[13] Robinson recounted:

> I used to be on the board of the Royal Ballet in England. Gillian and I had lunch one day and I asked, "How did you become a dancer?" When she was in school, she was really hopeless. And the school, in the 1930s, wrote to her parents, "We think Gillian has a learning disorder." She couldn't concentrate. She was always fidgeting. She went to see a specialist. She sat on her hands for 20 minutes while this man talked to her mother about all of the problems Gillian was having in school. And, at the end of it, because she was disturbing people, her homework was always late, and so on—little kid of eight. In the end, the doctor went and sat next to Gillian. "I listened to all of these things that your mother told me. I need to go speak to her privately. Wait here, we'll be back. We won't be very long." And as they went out of the room, he turned on the radio, and when they got out of the room, he said, "Just stand there and watch her." The minute they left the room, she said that she was on her feet, listening to the music. They watched for a few minutes and he turned to her mother and he said, "Mrs. Lynne, Gillian isn't sick, she's a dancer. Take her to a dance school."

Sadly, Gillian passed away in 2018, at the age of 92. But her legend lives on.

Be different

I had just arrived in Minneapolis after speaking at a wonderful event in São Paolo, Brazil. I checked into my hotel and unpacked in preparation for the next day's presentation. My body was telling me to go to sleep, but my mind was racing. Sleep wouldn't come, not for a while at least.

I cracked open my laptop to write. The room was dark, without windows. I remember the light from my screen seemed brighter than all the lights in the room. It should have been a great space for creative focus, and my mind was on fire. But it was a wildfire—my thoughts were all over the place, except where I needed them to be. To clear my mind, I took a break to wander the streets of downtown Minneapolis.

As I walked along 7th Street toward 1st Avenue on that warm fall Friday evening, I came upon the infamous rock venue First Avenue. Prince, one of my favorite artists of all time, played the club (then called Sam's) on March 9, 1981![14] Wow. I had to geek out for a minute and see the famous "Prince Star" along with the others of iconic stars who once played this storied location. Feeling inspired, I walked across the street to take a picture. As I was framing the shot, I noticed two billboards above the *First Avenue* marquee.[15]

I found myself, surprisingly, inspired yet again.

The billboards were part of Apple's latest campaign, *Behind the Mac*. I don't normally take pause for ads. I think we can all agree that our conscious and subconscious are overwhelmed with marketing messages 24/7. But this was different. I was mesmerized.

I'm pretty sure I looked like a weirdo on a busy night standing on a corner, contemplating these billboards. Maybe some people thought I was tripping on something psychedelic. But these billboards were artistically stunning. The composition, the physical lighting of the billboards, the black and white contrast of someone passionately and lovingly gazing into their MacBook was magnetic. The individuals *behind the Mac* clearly see something different than most of us do when we stare at our screens; they see a more beautiful world. And, they're creating it.

The billboard was an artistic statement as much as an ad, meant to evoke an emotional, personal, and aspirational response. It was a call to tap our creativity. I still visit the stills I took often when I sit down to do creative work.

This new campaign harkened back to Apple's famous *Think Different* ads.[16] They featured some of the greatest artists, adventurers, and geniuses of our time, such as Albert Einstein, Bob Dylan, Martin Luther King, Jr., Richard Branson, John Lennon and Yoko Ono, R. Buckminster Fuller, Thomas Edison, Muhammad Ali, Ted Turner, Maria Callas, Mahatma Gandhi, Amelia Earhart, Alfred Hitchcock, Martha Graham, Jim Henson (with Kermit the Frog), Frank Lloyd Wright, and Pablo Picasso.

Narrated by Richard Dreyfuss, the TV spot eases into an unforgettable tribute to counterculture norms and ideals. "Here's to the crazy ones," Dreyfuss begins in a masterful but soothing voice. "The misfits, the rebels, the troublemakers—the round pegs in the square holes. The ones who see things differently."

These icons, each in their own way, represented more than their achievements. They were inspired and inspiring in their life experiences, their failures, and their larger-than-life personas. They were innovators and trailblazers and they paved the way for others like them to continue the path they started. In doing so, they changed the world for the rest of us. But what also made it so relatable and inspiring was how it intentionally excluded a notable segment of the audience and an enormous potential market for PCs. It didn't seek to gain the attention of businesses aiming to increase workplace productivity. It didn't cultivate acceptance from IT or technology groups making big enterprise-wide purchases for organizations. No, it sought to connect with the dreamers, the doers, the would-be revolutionaries. It reminded them, us, that we have something to offer life beyond conformity.

And yet, we have been educated—and are still educating our children—out of distinctive flare.

To those who would have us become automatons, consider this. In this time of rampant technological advancement and market disruption, many jobs will be lost to automation. For example, in late 2017, the CEO of Deutsche Bank predicted that half of its workforce (97,000 employees) could be replaced by robots.[17] Separately, another survey shockingly asserted that "39% of jobs in the legal sector could be automated in the next 10 years.[18] And yet another shocker found that accountants have a 95% chance of losing their jobs to automation in the future."[19] And, the list goes on and on.

On the positive side, historically, with every technological advancement, new jobs are created. Incredible opportunity opens up for individuals to learn new skills and create in new ways. It is your mindset, the new in-demand skills you learn, and your creativity that will assure you a bright future in the age of automation.

This is not just my opinion. A thoughtful article in *Harvard Business Review* by Joseph Pistrui was titled, "The Future of Human Work Is Imagination, Creativity, and Strategy."[20] He cites research by McKinsey, which among many leading consultancies, is thoroughly studying the intersection of human and technological performance. In their research, they discovered that the more technical the work, the more replaceable it is by technology. However, work that requires imagination, creative thinking, analysis, and strategic thinking is not only more difficult to automate; it is those capabilities that are needed to guide and govern the machines.

The good news for you, even if you don't yet feel that you're particularly creative, is that creativity isn't just a gift to the fortunate. It can be learned.[21] We can all improve, grow, and develop the mental, physical, and emotional skills necessary to think different.

That process begins by rekindling our creative spirit.

Believe

REKINDLE

Creativity Is
the Fountain of Youth,
a Source of Innovation,
and the Secret
to Happiness

> "You can't use up creativity.
> The more you use, the more you have."
> - Maya Angelou

No matter how young or old we are, we can all rekindle our most youthful, unfettered, joyful creativity. Age and creativity are not bound to one another. Creativity is like an age-defying elixir.

The seemingly ageless actress Sophia Loren wisely said, "There is a fountain of youth: it is your mind, your talents, the creativity you bring to your life and the lives of people you love. When you learn to tap this source, you will truly have defeated age."[1] It keeps us young, sharp, optimistic, and enlightened.

"There is a fountain of youth: it is your mind, your talents, the creativity you bring to your life and the lives of people you love."

Take the case of Gary Marcus, a cognitive psychologist at New York University, who had always wondered, *what if* he learned how to play a musical instrument when he was younger.[2] Finally, one day, on the eve of his 40th birthday, he decided that he was going to learn to play the guitar. He began his immersion by playing *Guitar Hero*, a video game in which players match their rhythmic motions to the game's digital music sheet. In two years, practicing up to six hours per day, Marcus accelerated quickly through the awkward and struggling phases to experimenting, improvising, and composing his own music. His detailed experience was documented in his book, *Guitar Zero: The Science of Becoming Musical at Any Age*.

Rekindle

At the time of writing this chapter, I had orbited the sun 47 times. I hadn't realized how far away from the energizing heat of my youthful creative center I had traveled. I learned how to play the guitar when I was seven, played my first live show at 10, and wrote and recorded and toured with several albums worth of original material. I didn't appreciate fully at the time how special the thrill of playing was. As I wrote that line, I thought about the beautiful collection of guitars stuffed in a closet behind me that hadn't been able to sing because I hadn't made time for them. I stopped typing, walked into the closet, and stared at the guitar cases. I couldn't help but pull one out and start to play. Instantly, the musical passion I had repressed was rekindled.

We can all do this.

© Brian Solis

And we must, not only for the good of our performance at work, but for our happiness, and even for our health. In a study that examined the health benefits of creativity, Dr. Gene Cohen of George Washington University sought to understand how mental exercise is key to keeping the elderly young. "They want to be challenged, and science has shown that when you challenge older people, both physically and mentally, they do better," Cohen explained in an interview.[3] He also found that seniors who take on a creative challenge are healthier, they go to the doctor less, they are less depressed, and they suffer fewer injuries.

As life coach Triantafillia Memisakis writes,

As we grow up, some of us get scared out of being more creative. People judge us for it. So, we judge ourselves and censor our own creative expression. But, when we refuse to use our creativity . . . we suppress a very integral part of who we are. It's not just uncomfortable and unhelpful, when we suppress our creative impulses in this way, we can actually harm ourselves without even knowing it. Unused creativity warps into grief, rage, judgement, sorrow and shame. Not acknowledging or expressing our creative side can cause depression, uncertainty, stress and anxiety.[4]

Rekindle

On the flip side, the practice of creative tasks makes us happier. In a study published in 2016, psychologists found that spending time on creative goals is associated with a higher activated positive effect on that day and even the next.[5] You're also more likely to continue creative pursuits the next day. Dr. Tamlin Conner, a psychologist at New Zealand's University of Otago and the study's lead author, explains "Engaging in creative behavior leads to increases in well-being the next day, and this increased well-being is likely to facilitate creative activity on the same day." What's more, participants in the study also reported that they were "flourishing," which researchers defined as experiencing positive personal growth. "This finding suggests a particular kind of upward spiral for well-being and creativity," Dr. Conner noted. "Finding ways to encourage everyday creative activities, not just master works of art, could lead directly to increased well-being," she concluded.[6]

©Danielle Macinnes

It's time to reacquaint yourself with the artist formerly known as you. As my dear friend, entrepreneur, and on-air journalist Melissa Rowley once said, "You were born to create beautiful things because you were created from beauty. And, everything comes full circle."

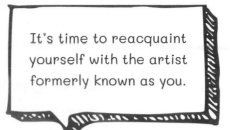

For some inspiration, let me share a brief story of one man who never lost touch with his inner child.

Conjuring a Magic Kingdom

Walt Disney not only said but demonstrated time and time again, "All our dreams can come true, if we have the courage to pursue them."

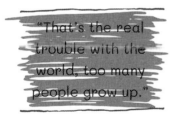

I think like everyone, when I was young, I wanted to be older. Now I'm working to reconnect to my youth, which is just one of the many reasons I'm so humbled and inspired by Walt Disney. He once said, "That's the real trouble with the world, too many people grow up. They forget. They don't remember what it's like to be 12 years old. They patronize, they treat children as inferiors. Well I won't do that."

©The editors of LIFE

Disney dedicated himself tirelessly to enchanting and making us believe in magical worlds, and yet can you believe that in 1919, at age 18, Disney was fired from the *Kansas City Star* newspaper because his editor felt he "lacked imagination and had no good ideas?"[7] Thankfully, Disney didn't believe him. Instead he discovered ways to transform drawings and storybooks into immersive animated worlds rich with characters we all cherish. The most famous of them all, Mickey Mouse, was introduced to the world on November 18, 1928, [8] when Disney was 27 years old. And, here we are today, still crazy about Mickey.

But Disney was by no means simply born with overflowing talent. He was as much a hard worker as an artist. He believed in highly disciplined goal setting, saying, "A person should set his goals as early as he can and devote all his energy and talent to getting there. With enough effort, he may achieve it. Or he may find something that is even more rewarding. But in the end, no matter what the outcome, he will know he has been alive."

"All you've got to do is own up to your ignorance honestly," he said, "and you'll find people who are eager to fill your head with information."

Disney had to overcome many obstacles. Receiving only an eighth-grade education, he chased after whatever he needed to know to pursue his dreams. He never stopped learning. He sought apprenticeships, taught himself animation, and invented new technologies, systems, and processes to bring his ideas to life until the day of his passing. "All you've got to do is own up to your ignorance honestly," he said, "and you'll find people who are eager to fill your head with information."

Throughout his life's work he faced naysayers who told him, "It cannot be done," and he suffered many setbacks. His first animation company, Laugh-O-gram Films, went bankrupt in 1921. At age 21, he left Kansas City for Southern California with $40 to his name. After arriving in Los Angeles, he sought work as a director of live action films in the silent film industry, but no one wanted to hire him.

Rekindle

So, instead he founded Disney Bros. Studio in Hollywood, along with his brother Roy. After developing the character of Mickey Mouse, then named Mortimer,[9] Disney made two animated shorts featuring him, *Plane Crazy* and *The Gallopin' Gaucho,* but failed to secure distribution for them. He moved right on to creating another Mickey film, the innovative *Steamboat Willie*, which brought sound to animation. That finally scored a distributor, and soon, Mickey Mouse surpassed Felix the Cat to become the world's most popular cartoon character.

©Skitterphoto

Later in life, Disney expressed gratitude for his failures and challenges. "All the adversity I've had in my life, all my troubles and obstacles, have strengthened me. . . . You may not realize it when it happens, but a kick in the teeth may be the best thing in the world for you."

In *How to Be Like Walt*, by Pat Williams with Jim Denney, Roy Disney shared his brother's secret to success: "If Walt had one great gift, it was that he kept his head down and kept trying. Over the years, he was told that his ideas were impractical, impossible and would never work. Walt proved the only way to get things done is by sticking to your ideas and your beliefs."

Rather than resting on his achievements, he kept pushing himself into new territory, his projects becoming ever more ambitious. Despite so many successes, he still faced doubters, including his brother Roy and wife Lillian. In 1934, he set out to produce his first feature-length animated film, *Snow White and the Seven Dwarfs*. The project was a big risk. The initial budget for the film was $250,000, which was 10 times that of the company's average *Silly Symphony* short. Justifiably frightened, Roy and Lillian attempted to dissuade Walt, but he paid no heed, mortgaging his house to help finance the production. As production costs skyrocketed to almost $1.5 million, an astronomical sum during the Great Depression, he kept his nerve—with good reason. The initial run of *Snow White* earned roughly $8 million, equivalent to about $134 million in today's terms.

Rekindle

©Haley Phelps

If the tools he needed for realizing his vision weren't available, he created them. He invented to pave the way for his other inventions. Disney's lists of firsts[10] and inventions[11] is practically countless, including the opening of the landmark Disneyland and Disney World, development of audio animatronics (electro-mechanical robots), the creation of People Movers and Monorails, the introduction of the world's first indoor shopping mall, the debut of switch-back and interactive lines, building fully enclosed attractions, many developments in ride innovation, and the creation of life-size models for cities of the future.

Disney referred to his creative process as *imagineering*, combining imagination with engineering.[12] He made magic by mixing imagination and determination. He captured the little hearts and big imaginations of children. He also helped former kids rekindle the magic of their youth. And now, we pass the magic of his creative kingdom onto our children, so that future generations too can hold on to heart, imagination, and invention. And as big kids looking to stay young, happy, and creative, we have to hold on to those dreams, and mix imagination and determination in our own life and work. That's the Disney ethic—stay true, stay dedicated. As he said, "The difference in winning and losing is most often not quitting."

©Travis Gergen

Rekindle

As we seek to reignite our creativity, we should prepare for some pain. Exercising our creativity unleashes happiness, but that doesn't mean it's always bliss. We'll almost surely encounter our own naysayers. The value of ideas is a matter of perspective. They are judged through the lenses of entrenched mindsets and cognitive biases. The way we think about our ideas and the way they're heard are often not in alignment, and expression of them pushes the boundaries of comfort for many of those in our lives. They may roll their eyes when we haul out our guitars or sit down to finally write that novel. It's an unfortunate reflex for many to belittle the creative endeavors of others, even of loved ones. It's okay. It's not you.

©Pressmaster

> "We don't look backwards for very long. We keep moving forward, opening up new doors and doing new things, because we're curious . . . and curiosity keeps leading us down new paths."

I find it helpful when I'm feeling the naysaying *grownup* Brian sneak up on me, telling me to stop pretending I'm creative, worrying about what the critics will say, to think of Walt Disney's 22 Academy Awards and seven Emmys. In 1964, he received the Presidential Medal of Freedom. But he still didn't believe in resting on his laurels. "Around here," he said of the thriving company he created, "we don't look backwards for very long. We keep moving forward, opening up new doors and doing new things, because we're curious . . . and curiosity keeps leading us down new paths."

As I've worked on this section about him, I've realized I want to be an imagineer when I grow up, or I should say, when I grow young again. What do you want to be?

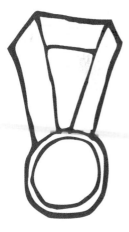

Rekindle

Color Outside the Lines Again: Get Back to the Roots of Your Creativity

Right now, go and find a Flux Capacitor, get in your DeLorean, hit 88 miles per hour and go back to a time when you were alive with overflowing creativity, ideas, aspirations and didn't like following the rules or being told what to do. Start a revolution within yourself.

(If you have no idea what a Flux Capcitator is and only a vague sense that I'm taking a nod from the movie *Back to the Future*, immediately put the film on your watch list.)

Remember when you were young. What did you enjoy doing as a child? What do you wish you could always have done but never did?

 **Start asking questions.** Part of following the rules is to not question them. But if you remember, one of your favorite questions to ask was, "Why?" We were curious. We honestly wanted to know why something existed, why we did things certain ways, why people were the way they were, why we couldn't do something, and so on. Asking questions should be just as important to us as adults. We should challenge ourselves all the time with exploratory questions such as "What if . . ." or "How can we . . . ?" Let your curiosity run wild.

 **Let yourself be silly.** Be a kid again and schedule playtime. Find time to do some of the things kids do. Play in a playground. Fly a kite. Build a sandcastle. Play tag or hide and seek. Watch cartoons and read children's books, even if you don't have children. Smile. Laugh. Take yourself to Disneyland!

Who cares if you look weird? I don't. Nor should you.

 **Shift positions from the impossible to seemingly possible.** Banish the phrase *we can't* and investigate the possibilities that seem improbable.

 **List three ideas every day.** Keep a running list of ideas you have each day, no matter how impossible, foolish, or grand. You don't have to stop at three. If ideas are flowing, bring them on. Visit the list every day as you add your new items and consider which of them you might now move to your actual to-do list.

Rekindle

 **Find a creative project.** You don't have to have talent in whatever you choose. Just find an outlet for exercising the right side of your brain. Paint, draw, doodle, write poetry or a book manuscript, script, or screenplay, play an instrument, cook, take pictures, make movies, or all of the above! Just create, regularly.

 **Express yourself in all you do.** Buy the clothes you love, stylish or not, pursue the activities that interest you, no matter how odd or boring they may seem to others; share your thoughts, even if they're contrarian or might seem wacky. Find your voice.

 **Be courageous.** Fearing risk or failure is the cancer of creativity, and taking chances is rocket fuel. The more chances you take, the more you learn, gain experience, and build confidence, and that becomes contagious!

As you have fun finding ways each day to rekindle your creativity, please join me on the next steps of the journey of lifescaling—reconnecting with your hopes and dreams, rediscovering what truly makes you happy, and crafting a clear understanding of your life purpose, that is, your purpose for this phase in the ongoing process of lifescaling.

RECONSIDER

Understanding
the Myth
of Happiness
Is the Key
to Happiness

"Most folks are usually about as happy as
they make their minds up to be."
– Abraham Lincoln

Tell me, who do you know who is *actually* willing to die for you? Chances are, when it comes down to it, most of us can only identify our parents and perhaps our siblings and/or spouse as *really* being prepared to die for us. So, why is it then, that we let so many people dictate the terms of our lives? Why do we allow the nebulous entity we call *society* define what will, or *should*, make us happy?

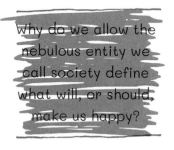

Why do we allow the nebulous entity we call society define what will, or should, make us happy?

Happiness has been defined many ways, but a widely accepted understanding is that it involves[1] frequently feeling positive emotions such as joy, interest, pride, love, and achievement and infrequently experiencing negative emotions such as sadness, anxiety, stress, and anger.[2] That definition doesn't distinguish, though, between *Happiness* and happiness.

Many of us mistake happiness, the pursuit of pleasure, for Happiness, the practice of pursuing a life rich in purpose.

Many of us mistake happiness, the pursuit of pleasure, for Happiness, the practice of pursuing a life rich in purpose.

After all, ours is a pleasure-seeking society; it teaches us to think that bursts of sensations are meaningful. Perhaps, you just enjoyed a wonderful meal, a recent vacation to your dream destination, a delicious bottle of wine, fantastic sex, or were surprised with a bonus at work. Who doesn't love those things? However, their temporary *happiness* effects are like those of chemical stimulants, and they soon wear off.

When we focus on these pleasurable stimulants, we tend to end up making mental lists of all the things we think we need to get and do in order to be happy. "If I just had this, this, and this . . .

That's the H/happiness trap. What makes it dangerous is that the things we think we want are so often not those we actually need. So, having those things will only give you a delusion of pleasure, which often does not actually even feel positive. We find ourselves living a charade, trying to convince ourselves, and others, we're loving our life when we're actually increasingly disturbed by our dissatisfaction.

Reconsider

©Matthew Henry

Ask yourself, have you ever craved attention, validation, recognition, approval, all as a means to feel a sense of happiness? We do this because we feel something is missing in our lives, and we've been conditioned to believe that if others see us as interesting, talented, and successful, we'll be happy with ourselves. But let me ask you, how much *unhappiness* has the lack of these things caused you?

It's perverse; we put our happiness in the hands of others, even of those we don't know. Social media has intensified this problem. Someone I don't even know retweeted my message! Yay! More than 1,000 strangers have read my review! *Awesome*!!! Except that Happiness isn't a zero-sum game. You don't win it by being more impressive, well liked, or successful than others. And the world, or someone in your life, doesn't win by taking happiness away from you. We can all make as much of it as we set our minds to, and we can live with it even in the tough times.

We are so intent to have positive feelings, but emotions are always fleeting, like hits of a drug. As soon as the hits of elation dissipate, we feel a lack of happiness again. True happiness is not a matter of a chemical rush.

Psychological research shows that the pursuit of happiness can actually make you less happy.[3] I've seen many variations and interpretations of that research while developing the lifescale methodology. The key to a more satisfying and fulfilling

> The key to a more satisfying and fulfilling life, according to experts, is the pursuit of meaning and having meaning in your life.

life, according to experts, is the pursuit of meaning and having meaning in your life. In his book, *Authentic Happiness*,[4] Martin E.P. Seligman, PhD, shared, "Meaning comes from belonging to and serving something beyond yourself and from developing the best within you."

Our desire to have enviable things and to feel approved of, liked, or even admired is entirely normal. It's human. We evolved that way. It's not our fault, and blaming ourselves isn't the point. But if we want to get out of the H/happiness trap, we have to appreciate that honest to goodness Happiness is not a matter of the pleasure we take from the stuff we have, the socially approved satisfaction we seek, the rush of temporary escape from our challenges we get from a fun night out or a scary movie, or a matter of others' views of us.

> Happiness is within our power, in our hands, because it is not a fleeting feeling that will inevitably dissipate; it's a process, a journey.

Reconsider

Authentic happiness is the result of a mindset. It follows from the adoption of the belief that happiness is within our power, in our hands, because it is not a fleeting feeling that will inevitably dissipate; it's a process, a journey. Our happiness is not tied to what other people think of us or even how they make us feel. True Happiness is rooted in how we see ourselves and the quest we are on. It flows from a sense of appreciation of how richly meaningful life can be, which allows us to be grateful for the experiences it offers, good and bad—though appreciating the bad will probably take some time.

The key is to seek the pleasures that contribute to true Happiness, to a sense that we are making a valuable contribution in life and pursuing what really matters to us. The meaningful and positive pursuit of happiness is also the foundation for this. We have to shed ourselves of devotion to the misleading notions that have kept us in the trap. The state of your mind, heart, and spirit is a result of whatever it is you set your mind to and whatever it is that you strive toward.

©Pete Linforth

We tend to think of happiness as a goal. But Happiness is not a destination. It's a way of life. You don't just land upon an island of happiness and say, "Yes! I've arrived; now I will forever be happy!" Happiness isn't something we have to search high and low for. The secret to real, bona fide Happiness is to accept that it's already inside you. You just have to know what it is that makes *you* Happy. You have to know what it is you are genuinely interested in achieving, and what it is you truly value.

A big part of why living with Happiness can be so difficult is that we haven't undergone deeply introspective examination of ourselves and what we value. What *really* makes you happy? Can you honestly say? What is it you're truly thankful for? I, for one, never really thought further about this than believing I took pleasure from the false gods I worshipped.

We can all live with authentic Happiness; it just takes some committed work.

Dr. Sonja Lyubomirsky, a leading researcher in the field of happiness studies and author of *The Myths of Happiness*, writes, "You can make yourself happier just like you can make yourself lose weight. But like eating differently and going to the gym faithfully, you have to put in the effort every day. You have to stay with it."

Understanding that we can choose to live with authentic Happiness, every day if we keep up the work, really deeply absorbing the truth of that and believing it, is the next step in lifescaling.

To choose Happiness we have to first know what actually makes us Happy, what we value in our lives, where we are going and why. Clarifying all of that begins with a deeply thoughtful consideration of our values.

VALUE

Your Values
Guide You to
Your Purpose

> "Your beliefs become your thoughts. Your thoughts
> become your words. Your words become your actions.
> Your actions become your habits. Your habits become
> your values. Your values become your destiny."
> – Ghandi

When's the last time you examined your core values? With full transparency, I can tell you that I never really considered what they are, or should be, in any formal way that would help to ensure they were guiding me through life. Then, in a miracle of fortunate timing, I was asked about my values twice in two days, in two different states by two people in two unrelated conversations. Their questions served as a catalyst for my own deep exploration of my values.

From New York to Boston: The Serendipity of Rediscovering the Value of Values

There I was, sitting again at a lounge I had visited a mere hour before at New York's LaGuardia airport. I had boarded my flight to Boston only to deplane due to severe weather at Logan airport that had shut down all flights. I was exhausted from the week of travel but also still buzzing from an incredibly inspiring conversation the night before with dear friends that lasted well into the morning. Heightening the experience, our conversation took place on a New York rooftop with a marvelous view on an abnormally warm summer evening.

Since I found myself with an abundance of time, I decided not to work and instead replayed in my mind some of the memorable moments from the evening before. The part of the conversation that really stuck with me was about personal values and decision-making and how easy it is to lose touch with their importance in guiding our lives in purposeful directions. One individual in particular found himself on a completely different life journey than he anticipated following a series of misguided decisions. His moral compass, he shared, hadn't been consulted before each poor decision.

Those missteps led him to realize he was in need of deep reflection and enlightenment. He sought to discover the reasons behind his bad choices. Some deep introspection revealed the key to his future and the answers to his past. He had lost touch with his personal values. In doing so, he also lost touch with the underlying fabric of life and the essence of happiness.

©Luis Eusebio

He went on to explore his values and built on them to redefine his life goals and has since reset his compass, living a renewed and happier life.

Four hours later, I finally boarded my flight to Boston and soon arrived at Logan airport. I was worried that I was going to miss a chance to see a special friend from Slovenia who was visiting Boston for work and was leaving the next day. I hadn't seen her for two years and it would probably be another two years until I would have an opportunity to see her again. To my great good fortune, I got there in time to enjoy a glass of champagne with her.

Almost instantly, she observed that I looked "really different" and "really happy" and wanted to know what was new in my life. To my surprise, I responded, "Wow. Thank you. You know? A lot has changed." I shared that I had been working on this book and had been developing my focus and rekindling my creativity.

She listened thoughtfully and then surprised me again by responding, "May I ask, what are your values and have they changed?"

In New York, I was a listener, allowing a friend to share a deeply personal story of values and their importance in guiding one's life. Now, I was the one who needed to share, and I decided to really open up.

I answered honestly, "I don't know." I told her that I had just had a very thought-provoking conversation about values the day before, and I divulged that I was trying to re-center my life, unlock my creativity, and chart a course toward happiness.

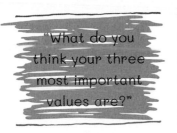
"What do you think your three most important values are?"

She then shared a recent experience she felt would help me. I was so compelled by her story that I wrote this section on my flight home from Boston to San Francisco the next day.

"What do you think your three most important values are?" she asked.

Before I could respond, she added, "You won't believe that I bet they're the three everyone has on their list."

With a moment of reflection, I offered that my top three were "family, love, and happiness."

She smiled and replied, "Yep, those were at the top of my list, too."

She went on to say that these are on everyone's list because we all have experiences that teach us that if we lose touch with their importance to us, we lose our sense of direction in life. We begin making bad choices that pull us even further away from what truly matters to us.

She then said with excitement, "I have to tell you about an experience I recently had in Europe. I went through an unforgettable values exercise that is helping me center my life around what's important . . . what's missing in my world." The exercise is basic, yet profound. Following our heartening conversation, after some research I set out to simplify it a little, to craft a process for us to go through together.

Value

©Ruediger Theiselmann

The value of values

We should start with defining what values are and why they're important. Values guide our behavior. They represent the underlying fabric of how, what, and who surrounds you and how you navigate life's daily challenges and opportunities. Whether it's your friendships, relationships, art, work, partnerships, financial management, or how you spend your time and resources, values are (or at least, they're supposed to be) the guideposts that help you live your truly best life. Values provide the warmth in the best of times and light in the most difficult. They are what keeps you true to yourself. Your beliefs become your thoughts and your thoughts become your reality.

When I sat down to consider my values, I discovered my understanding of them was nebulous at best. As I reflected on them, I realized that the character I believed I emanated and the character who really showed up in important life events were in conflict. I hadn't been seeing that. As a result, I hurt people close to me and made poor business decisions.

Looking back over the past several years, I was stunned that I hadn't seen how out of alignment with my true values my life had gotten. We don't see that because we lose our way small steps at a time. As with my friend in New York, I'd made a series of missteps that pulled me further and further away from my moral center.

Value

Defining What Is Right, not What's Right for Right Now

American humorist, author, and screenwriter Leo C. Rosten once observed,[1] "I cannot believe that the purpose of life is to be 'happy.' I think the purpose of life is to be useful, to be responsible, to be honorable, to be compassionate. It is, above all, to matter: to count, to stand for something, to have made some difference that you lived at all." I would just add that by living in the values-driven way he describes, we can achieve the happiness we hope for.

> I cannot believe that the purpose of life is to be 'happy.'

To gain clarity about the values you want to guide you, and then build on that awareness to reset your own compass, grab some paper and go through the following exercise, writing down your answers. The act of getting them down on the page helps to reveal the messages within them.

Step 1:

Start by identifying times in your life when you were happiest.

- Write it out—what were you doing or what did you achieve?

- Who were you with and/or what were the surrounding circumstances?

- What factors contributed to that happiness?

- What values would you associate with these experiences?

Step 2: Identify the saddest, angriest, and most desolate moments in your life.

- What happened?

- Who were you with and/or what were the surrounding circumstances?

- What factors contributed to these feelings?

- How did you (or did you not) move on and what did you learn?

- What values would you associate with moving on?

Step 3:

Assemble the values from steps 1 and 2 and list them in a matrix-style format (you're going to move them around in a bit).

Step 4:

Outline a list of your additional personal values that may not have come up yet. The list can include as many as you want. Don't worry about putting them in any order; we'll organize them in a later step. To help with this, you can consult this list of common values. If you don't see a core value of yours, add it!

Abundance	Excellence	Piety
Accountability	Excitement	Positivity
Accuracy	Expertise	Practicality
Achievement	Exploration	Preparedness
Adventurousness	Expressiveness	Professionalism
Advocacy	Fairness	Prudence
Altruism	Faith	Quality
Ambition	Family	Relationships
Assertiveness	Fidelity	Reliability
Attractiveness	Fitness	Resourcefulness
Balance	Fluency	Responsibility
Being the best	Focus	Resilience
Belonging	Freedom	Restraint
Boldness	Friendships	Results-oriented
Brilliance	Fun	Rigor
Calmness	Generosity	Security
Carefulness	Goodness	Self-actualization
Caring	Grace	Self-control
Challenge	Growth	Selflessness
Cheerfulness	Happiness	Self-reliance
Clear-mindedness	Hard Work	Sensitivity
Commitment	Health	Serenity
Community	Helping Society	Service
Compassion	Holiness	Shrewdness
Competitiveness	Honesty	Simplicity
Consistency	Honor	Soundness
Contentment	Humility	Speed
Continuous	Humor	Spontaneity
Improvement	Inclusiveness	Stability

Contribution	Independence	Strategic
Control	Ingenuity	Strength
Cooperation	Inner Harmony	Structure
Correctness	Innovation	Success
Courtesy	Inquisitiveness	Support
Creativity	Insightfulness	Teamwork
Credibility	Inspiration	Temperance
Curiosity	Intelligence	Thankfulness
Daring	Intellectual Status	Thoroughness
Decisiveness	Intuition	Thoughtfulness
Democraticness	Joy	Timeliness
Dependability	Justice	Tolerance
Determination	Leadership	Traditionalism
Devoutness	Legacy	Trustworthiness
Diligence	Love	Truth-seeking
Discipline	Loyalty	Understanding
Discretion	Making a	Uniqueness
Diversity	difference	Unity
Dynamism	Mastery	Usefulness
Economy	Merit	Vision
Effectiveness	Mindful	Vitality
Efficiency	Obedience	Versatility
Elegance	Openness	Vision
Empathy	Order	Warmth
Enjoyment	Originality	Wealth
Enthusiasm	Parenting	Well-being
Equality	Patriotism	Wisdom
	Perfection	Zeal

Source: Scott Jeffrey[2]

Image source: Carnegie Mellon University[3]

Step 5:

Organize your values by themes, and try to limit the groupings to a maximum of five. For example, values such as accountability, responsibility, and timeliness are all related. Values such as learning, growth, and development also relate to each other, as do connection, belonging, and intimacy.

Step 6:

Select one value in each group that you think best represents the common thread that ties them together. Maybe for the learning, growth, and development cluster, for example, that would be growth. Note: There is no wrong answer here. The right answer is simply what feels right to you.

Step 7:

Select a subset of all the values you've listed that are the most important to you. This helps you focus on the aspects of your life that are both most in alignment and the most out of whack, and to prioritize the changes you want to implement.

Value

It's easy to align with many of the values you see in the sample list, but too many make action nearly impossible. For most people, the magic range is between 5 and 10. Once you've selected yours, take the prioritization a step further by ranking them in order of importance. Revisit this list over the next day or so and make sure it still rings true.

This part of the exercise can be surprisingly difficult, so here are some questions that will help:

- Which values are consistent with your best memories and those that helped you through your worst of times?

- What values are essential to your lifescale?

- What values are essential to supporting what you stand for?

- If you were in a hospital bed, what values would you hold most dearly if you were to ever get out?

Step 8:

For each value, write a short description of the actions by which you want to fulfill it in your life. These are your values commitments.

To clarify, the following are the statements I wrote:

 Mindful: To be more aware and more present. To be less open to distraction and more vested and amazing in the moment.

 Family: To be active in the lives of my family, to carve out time to help them and invest in our relationships to grow and thrive.

 Love: To feel loved and give love unselfishly and unconditionally, as well as passionately.

 Creative: To unleash my imagination and passion through creativity in ways that consistently and continually give me joy and inspire those around me.

Value

Friendship: To give and grow through the meaning of a more selective ecosystem of friends— and to help an extended group of friends grow through the power of the communities where I contribute.

 Abundance: To earn and save modestly to provide for a greater array of life choices that benefit my family and friends.

 Health: To live a healthier life that respects my body, mind, and spirit.

 Thankful: To live life less selfishly and more gratefully.

 Truthful: To live a sincere and honest life and earn trust in all I do.

 Learn: To never believe I've learned all I can and to live a more curious and humble life.

Now, it's your turn.

Step 9:

Roy Disney once said, "It's not hard to make decisions when you know what your values are." Keep your set of value commitments somewhere close to hand, maybe on the wall by your desk, in your purse or wallet, or saved on your device of choice.

As you proceed with the next steps of the lifescaling process, revisit the list periodically. Doing so will help you immediately begin making decisions and implementing changes in your life that get you in better alignment with the way in which you truly, deeply aspire to live. The commitments will also guide you in formulating a clear and powerfully motivating statement of your life's purpose for this leg of your journey.

Before we get to crafting your purpose statement, though, it's important to gain clarity about the ways in which you're being pulled away from living as you authentically want. That requires building deeper self-awareness and grappling with the baggage you've been carrying about what success looks like, which has been weighing you down.

Value

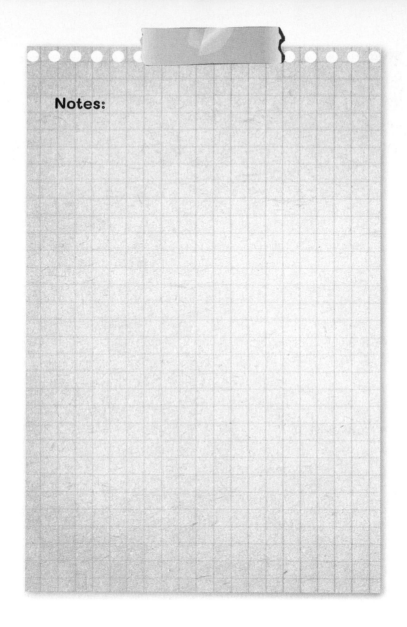

Notes:

REORIENT

From What about Me to What Can I Do?

> "Yesterday I was clever, so I wanted to change the world.
> Today I am wise, so I am changing myself."
> – Rumi

Professor Srikumar Rao[1] is often described as a *happiness guru* and a *modern-day-Yoda*[2] (to which I instinctively reacted with an eye roll). But when I checked out his work, he quickly convinced me he has vitally important insights about self-awareness. He helped me understand how breaking out of the prison of egocentric thinking is crucial to reorienting ourselves to living more in accord with our values and clarifying our purpose.

You may want to watch his TED talk; he is an incredibly engaging speaker, with much wisdom to offer. One point he makes especially jumped out at me.

Dr. Rao contends that we live in a "me-centered universe." I call it the *egosystem*. Life today, especially all of our distracting technology and the media that wants to hog our attention, seduces us into what I refer to as *accidental narcissism*— thinking about ourselves almost constantly, even subconsciously when we don't intend to.

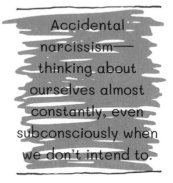

Accidental narcissism— thinking about ourselves almost constantly, even subconsciously when we don't intend to.

As Dr. Rao points out, no matter what's happening in our lives, we tend to ask ourselves, "What's the impact on me?" As he said at Mindvalley Extraordinary Summit, "It doesn't take very long to bring the conversation, in your head, to what's the impact on me? Your spouse gets a great job offer, gee, how is this going to affect our relationship?"

We need to break out of this me-centered thinking if we are to begin living more in accord with our authentic values and with a clear and strong sense of purpose. Dr. Rao describes the connection to purpose this way:

Here's something you should know about the 'me-centered universe.' That is where you spend the vast majority of your time. If that is where you predominately live, you are going to live, by and large, a mediocre, frustrated existence, punctuated with flashes of pleasure. That's just the way it is.

The only way out of that . . . is if you can find a cause which is bigger than you are, a cause that brings a greater good to a greater community, you have tremendous flexibility in defining the greater good and greater community . . . but, unless you can find something that is important to you, to which you can subsume your whole life, or at least a big chunk of it, and which does something to benefit a larger group, you're going to live a mediocre existence.

Reorient

Breaking free is, he admits, very difficult. But he ended his presentation with good news: "Even a modest stride will have a tremendous impact on your life."[3]

"Here's something you should know about the 'me-centered universe, you are going to live, by and large, a mediocre, frustrated existence, punctuated with flashes of pleasure."

How do we begin? The first step is to come to terms with the fact that how we see ourselves is different from how we really are, and that what we promise ourselves about how we'll conduct our lives is different from the way in which we often do. Our *what about me* focus prevents us from seeing accurately how we're acting and reinforces our self-biased beliefs.

Everything you look for and all that you perceive has a way of proving whatever you believe.

We tend to justify our mistakes and dodgy behavior with self-serving rationalizations and to see what's happening to us and the behavior of those around us through a self-interested lens. This is, again, not our fault. We evolved this way, and a degree of self-interest is important to thriving. But we've got to get the balance right.

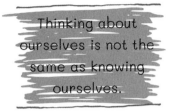

Thinking about ourselves is not the same as knowing ourselves.

To see more accurately, we have to cultivate self-awareness.

That doesn't mean just thinking about ourselves. Thinking about ourselves is not the same as knowing ourselves. Often, we invest in the former, without ever getting to know who we really are and why. As such, we can't envision who we need to be and how to get there.

©Oscar Keys

Tasha Eurich, organizational psychologist and author of *Insight: The Surprising Truth About How Others See Us, How We See Ourselves, and Why the Answers Matter More Than We Think*,[4] found in her research on self-awareness that 95% of those she studied thought they were self-aware, while only 10–15% actually *were* self-aware, which she interpreted as meaning around 80% were lying to themselves about lying to themselves.

This is a great shame, because there are so many benefits to being self-aware. Psychologist Daniel Goleman, author of the influential book *Emotional Intelligence*, sees self-awareness as a foundation for emotional intelligence—the ability to monitor your own emotions as well as the emotions of others, to differentiate and identify various emotions correctly, and to use that emotional information to guide your thinking and behavior with intention.[5]

Additional benefits are that self-aware people are generally more positive thinkers. They are also more compassionate with themselves and others and

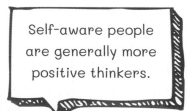

Self-aware people are generally more positive thinkers.

they tend to act more consciously, rather than passively and reactively. This fosters psychological well-being, and more values-driven, purposeful living.

It also helps people be more successful in their work. A Green Peak Partners and Cornell University study[6] of 72 executives at companies with revenue ranging from $50 million to $5 billion found that a "high self-awareness score was the strongest predictor of overall success."

> Most of us spend almost half our time in our day-to-day lives operating on automatic pilot. We're unconscious of what we're doing and feeling, as our mind wanders everywhere but the here and now.

Yet most of us spend almost half our time in our day-to-day lives operating on automatic pilot. We're unconscious of what we're doing and feeling, as our mind wanders everywhere but the here and now, according to psychologists Matthew Killingsworth and Daniel T. Gilbert of Harvard.[7]

Introspection about What Not Why

In a presentation on this subject at TEDxMileHigh, psychologist Tasha Eurich offered powerful insight about the key mistake most of us make when we try to become more self-aware. "The approach you're using to examine your thoughts, your feelings and your motive, you know, introspection. Well, you're probably doing it . . . *totally wrong*. There is a reason so few of us are self-aware," she said.[8]

Her research uncovered that our efforts to become more self-aware through introspection actually make us more stressed and depressed. She learned that in trying to take control of our lives in this way, we ironically feel less in control of our lives. Her realization was that self-analysis "can trap us in a mental hell of our own making."

Reorient

The problem, she has found, is that we ask the wrong question. When we're trying to become self-aware, we ask *why*? We're generally focused on trying to figure out why something happened to us—*why me*?

"Why is this happening to me?"

"Why do I feel this way?"

"Why is everyone out to get me?"

"Why can't things just go right for me?"

"Why can't I focus?"

"Why can't I create the way I used to?"

This seems perfectly logical to us. After all, we learned from an early age that if we want to understand things, we should ask why questions. Asking why is part of developing our sense of ourselves as independent people, beginning the process of understanding the way the world works. Most children go through a phase as they're developing their awareness of themselves as an independent being, generally between age two and three, of incessantly asking *why*. As a parent I can say it's a great phase—until it's not. All the why questions start to drive you crazy, in part because you know so few answers!

Wanting to know why things are as they are is a sign of taking responsibility for making our way in the world. Unfortunately, when it comes to self-awareness, though, asking why works against us. Tasha Eurich has learned, "When we ask why, it doesn't lead us to the truth about ourselves, it leads us away from it." We get so caught up in looking backward, trying to establish a causal chain of events that have led us to where we are, that we're not focusing on the possibilities of the present and how we can move forward. In other words, we get stuck in the *egosystem*.

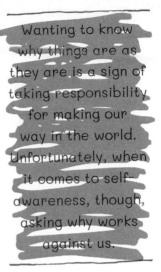

Wanting to know why things are as they are is a sign of taking responsibility for making our way in the world. Unfortunately, when it comes to self-awareness, though, asking why works against us.

Eurich says that we have to break out of the why trap.

In her research she found that those who are truly self-aware share something interesting in common. They don't ask *why*. Instead, they're focused on *what*. They ask themselves questions like:

"What's important to me?"

"What situations make me feel terrible and what do they have in common?"

"What is my purpose in life, right now, and what will it take for me to fulfill it?"

©Guillaume Flandre

Eurich believes that whereas asking *why* has us looking in the rearview mirror, which blocks or misdirects self-awareness, asking *what* moves us forward productively, helping us arrive at answers that allow for positive introspection and self-assessments.

To keep our minds from reverting back to the *why* and the *what about me*?! from *what* requires mindfulness, the ability to be aware of our thoughts and to redirect them. If we don't build up our mindfulness muscles, then, as novelist David Foster Wallace said in a famous commencement speech, we inevitably get caught up again in the egosystem:

> If I don't make a conscious decision about how to think and what to pay attention to, I'm gonna be pissed and miserable every time ... because my natural default setting is the certainty that situations ... are really all about me.[9]

The good news is that cultivating mindfulness is a source of great pleasure—the fulfilling, meaningful sort of pleasure that enriches our lives. We also know a great deal about how to do it. The next step in our lifescaling journey is spending a little time getting mindful.

©Lesly Juarez

SILENCE

Chapter 9

A Mental Wonderland Is Yours for the Creating— and Playing

> "Silence is a source of great strength."
> – Lay Tzu

A disciple and his master were walking through the woods. The disciple felt disturbed by the fact that his mind was in a constant state of agitation, and he asked his master: "Why are most people's minds restless? What can be done to calm the mind?" The master looked at the disciple, smiled, and said, "I will tell you a story."

An elephant was standing by a tree eating its leaves. A small fly came and flew up to him, making an unpleasant buzzing sound near his ear, and the elephant flapped his ears to scare it away. But a short time later, the fly came back. The elephant once again shook his ears, but the fly kept returning, over and over again.

After many failed attempts to scare the fly away, the elephant turned to it and asked, "Why are you so agitated and noisy? Why can't you stay in one place for a while?"

The fly responded, "I am attracted to what I see, hear, or smell. My five senses scream at me about everything around me and I cannot help myself. What is your secret, elephant? How can you stay so calm and quiet?"

The elephant stopped eating and said, "My five senses do not direct my attention. I have control of my attention and I can direct it where I wish. This helps me immerse myself in what I am doing and therefore to keep my mind calm and focused. When I am eating, I am totally immersed in eating. In this way, I can enjoy my food and better chew it. I control my attention and not the other way around, and this helps me to be calm."

Silence

In order to chart your path to a more focused and rewarding life, and to stay the course as you develop new life habits, you have to take control of your mind.

Why do we allow the nebulous entity we call society define what will, or should, make us happy?

Don't Let the Present Slip Away

One of the harmful effects of all of our distractions is that we are so rarely living entirely in the moment. Far too much of our time is spent worrying about where we are rather than appreciating where we are. Martin Farquhar Tupper once quipped,[1] "I remember the old man who said he had had a great many troubles in his life, but the worst of them never happened."

©Boram Kim

Focusing on what was or might be makes us unable to get so much enjoyment that we could be experiencing from where we are while we are there. Anyone we're with knows we're not really with them, unless they're distracted and not in the moment, as well. When you're at work, you may often think of your last vacation or one that's upcoming or an important life event. At the same time, when you're on that vacation or at the event, you may have pervading thoughts of work, deadlines, or projects that await you. How ironic!

The distractions of notifications, texts, emails, and posts are only part of the problem. Our mental chatter is also constantly diverting our attention from the present.

What do I mean by mental chatter? It's the incessant stream of thoughts or the relentless barraging of the voice in your head; the constant internal monologue that ebbs and flows in and out of your consciousness. While some of this jabbering is helpful, maybe by reminding us of a scheduled call we were about to miss, or bringing us a great idea in a flash of insight, most of our mental chatter is negative and unproductive.

Mental chatter is the incessant stream of thoughts or the relentless barraging of the voice in your head; the constant internal monologue that ebbs and flows in and out of your consciousness.

Silence

Take a moment right now to check in with your mental chatter. Maybe you're thinking about something you need to do later. Maybe you're contemplating an email you need to send or read, or perhaps you're worrying about an upcoming appointment. Your mind is trying to help you, but it's churning up attention energy that you need for focused productivity. Mental chatter is not only counterproductive; it's literally exhausting as it depletes our brain fuel. What's more, it leads to many unhealthy behaviors, including getting caught up in overanalyzing, holding on to and reliving past occurrences, and fostering damaging emotional states.[2] The Mayo Clinic describes the emotional effects this way:

Spending too much time planning, problem-solving, daydreaming, or thinking negative or random thoughts can be draining. It can also make you more likely to experience stress, anxiety and symptoms of depression.

©Chairulfajar

When we're centered in the present moment, we quiet the chatter. It's still there, but we don't notice it. The calming effect is uplifting and restorative; our energy is renewed.

To get a taste of the joy of being in the now, *please stop thinking for a moment*. I mean right now. Stop the mindless noise. Are you worrying about whether you can do it? That's just more useless chatter. Tell the voice in your head, will you be quiet for a moment, please?

Now, we're going to take a quick mental break; I'm going to do this with you because I love this simple practice. If you find at any point that the voice starts chattering again, just tell it to please be quiet again and start over.

- Set your timer for 60 seconds.
- Turn off all distractions and ambient noise you're in control of.
- Think about absolutely nothing except this exercise.
- Hold your breath for five seconds.
- Exhale loudly!
- Then, breathe deeply, In through your nose and out through your mouth, holding it for a second.
- Watch your mind.
- Put this book down and continue.

How did you do? Honestly, it took me a few times to get it. The funny thing is, as I tried to calm my mind, I even thought of things to add to the initial set of steps in the exercise above, which broke the spell of calm. But after fine-tuning the list, and with several more attempts, I finally got it. And, the feeling of calm was so wonderful that I've made it part of my daily life, doing it several times a day, and at any moment that I'm feeling particularly distracted or distressed.

One of the benefits of this quick exercise is that you're bringing oxygen to the brain,[3] which your brain cells crave. It's like a refreshing drink of cold water when you're dehydrated. Your muscles relax, no longer tensed by stress and anxiety, and you can direct your attention to only what you want to focus on in the present moment. You are more productive and you're happier.

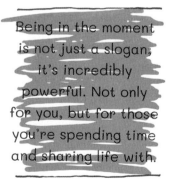
Being in the moment is not just a slogan; it's incredibly powerful. Not only for you, but for those you're spending time and sharing life with.

Being in the moment is not just a slogan; it's incredibly powerful. Not only for you, but for those you're spending time and sharing life with. It's like an elixir of connection. Your presence is charismatic. The fact that you're attentive makes people feel heard, understood, and special, and that gift of being truly with them strengthens relationships. That, in turn, boosts success and happiness.

A study conducted in 2010 found that 47% of people's waking hours were generally spent thinking about something other than what those surveyed were doing in the moment. The researchers, Matthew A. Killingsworth and Daniel T. Gilbert of Harvard University,[4] learned that when the participants' minds were aimlessly mind-wandering, they felt largely unhappy. When they were focused on the present moment, they were their happiest. And that was true even if the activity they were engaged in was unpleasant.[5]

The Art of *Now*, not *Next*

Don't let the past and future rob you of the power of being in the present. Let your mind give you time back.

Both the magic and the conundrum of time is that it always passes, and it never comes back. We only have so much of it. We should savor it. But through distraction in all of its forms, we're literally letting time, precious time, slip away from us. We're so busy rushing through life, devoting our time to dispiriting and meaningless pursuits that don't give back to us that we lose our sense of how much time is passing.

Too often, we realize only at the end of our careers how much of our time we've wasted this way. It's often said that at the end of our lives, no one wishes they had worked more. Well ditto that for worrying more, or procrastinating more, or scrolling through more Instagram photos.

> At the end of our lives, no one wishes they had worked more.

We can fix this. We can learn to live in the moment by cultivating mindfulness, a state of active, open, intentional attention on the present[6]—of being with your thoughts, conscious of your surroundings, and aware of your feelings and bodily sensations. You're also experiencing the present without the obsessive interpretation and judgment of your inner voice. You've turned the volume down on. Instead of letting the present flow past while barely noticing it, you intentionally awaken to the experience of the moment, appreciating it, challenges and all.

©Camila Cordeiro

Cultivating mindfulness has a wealth of benefits. "Depression lives in the past and anxiety lives in the future," Dr. Elyssa Barbash describes of mindfulness. "Alternately, calmness and peace of mind live in the present."[6] Mindful people are generally happier, more secure, empathetic, and alert. They're more relaxed, sleep better, experience professional burnout less frequently and are generally more grateful, which research shows is one of the most powerful sources of authentic Happiness. Their self-esteem is higher, leading to less anxiety about how they're performing and what others are thinking of them. Their attention is stronger and they have good defenses against unproductive impulses, like binging and the endless scroll. Mindfulness is also an enabler of creativity because it frees your mind from the energy depletion of chatter and distraction, allowing you to concentrate it on your creative problem-solving.[7]

With all of the virtues and life advantages of mindfulness, why aren't we better at practicing it? One reason is that many of us believe we are actually in the moment when we're not. After all, we're conscious of what we're doing, and we're most often engaged in at least some of what we should be focusing on. We may occasionally snap out of an episode of deep daydreaming and surprise ourselves with how out of the moment we were, but for the most part, we're aware of where we are and what we're doing in the moment. That awareness, though, is just one train of thought most of the time, and we're constantly toggling from it to our distractions and chatter.

Ellen Langer, a psychologist at Harvard and author of *Mindfulness*, describes the challenge this way, "Everyone agrees it's important to live in the moment, but the problem is how. When people are not in the moment, they're not there to know that they're not there."

Fortunately, there are lots of simple—and enjoyable— ways to foster mindfulness.

> Mindfulness is the outcome of building skills and strengthening the mind and body in the right place.

According to Laurie J. Cameron, author of *The Mindful Day*, "Mindfulness is the outcome of building skills and strengthening the mind and body in the right place. We strengthen the pre-frontal cortex, the part of the brain associated with attention, planning, and goal setting. We also train in deepening self-awareness, self-management, communication, motivation, and empathy."[8]

That may sound challenging, but I've sorted through the vast literature on mindfulness training to give you a set of fun ways to get started with strengthening your mindfulness muscles.

Embrace a beginner's mindset. Shake up how you go about your most basic autopilot habits. This is a way of making you more aware of what you're doing. For example, reverse the process of how you towel yourself dry when you get out of the shower. Try writing a short, motivational note to yourself with your non-writing hand. Travel to work by a different route and pay close attention to the surroundings: the beauty of the trees by the road, the new restaurant that looks appealing, or the gym you've been hearing about. Before you take a bite of your next meal or take a drink of your beverage of choice, smell it; take a good long breath in and savor the aroma. As you taste it, deconstruct the flavors, and focus for a bit on each of them. Don't worry while doing this that you'll look totally weird. It's likely no one will notice. Most people are too distracted!

Color. Maybe you've heard about the runaway popularity of adult coloring books and thought, what a silly way to spend time! Or maybe you're one of the legion of adults who've fallen in love with them. If so, bravo! Coloring is great for our minds. Art therapist Marygrace Berberian, the director of New York University's Art Therapy in Schools Program, explains that it is restorative because when we engage in a low-demand creative activity of this kind, our mind is calmed and drawn into a meditative state.[9] Coloring is also good for our creativity because it helps us tap into our inner child. So, pick up markers or crayons and a coloring book of your choice and go for it!

Practice un-self-consciousness. Self-consciousness holds us back from being in the moment. By worrying about how we're being perceived, or how our work will be received, we take our attention off the ball, so to speak, which leads us to flub the shot. This is the cause of the phenomenon of choking.

I've realized that I've sometimes been so self-conscious that I've sabotaged myself. One painful instance was in preparing for a televised presentation. As I sat down with the producers to go through the session, I panicked. Anxiety seemed to come over me out of nowhere. I unintentionally derailed the session because I didn't want to rehearse my part in front of everyone. I was worried they would have criticisms, which is, of course, exactly why you rehearse—to get better!

Make a commitment to yourself to pay close attention to whether you're being self-conscious, and whenever you hear that voice saying, "you sound stupid," or "they're going to hate this report," or "who are you kidding, you're going to make a mess of this," tell your mind to be quiet. If you're alone, go ahead and say it out loud. Then tell yourself, I've got this, so let's get back to it. Or come up with your own such mantra. You'll get better and better at circumventing your *me* focus and getting back in the moment.

Pay Attention to Your Breath. We did this earlier, so you know how powerful it is. Make this a regular habit; do it many times a day. Also, practice it whenever you're feeling anxious or stressed, whenever you find yourself reaching for your phone to check notices, and whenever you realize your mind is wandering. It's also another great way to break the grip of self-consciousness. If you do this regularly, even for just a minute, you will learn better how to catch yourself from getting pulled out of the moment and get your mind re-centered in the now.[10]

Practice Acceptance. One of the most well-supported findings in psychology is that by trying to escape from the difficulties life inevitably presents us with, we cause ourselves more pain. Much of our distraction is due to a willful, though often subconscious, desire to avoid things we fear, whether that's the exertion we'll have to put into a project, or ridicule we think we'll face if our work is deemed subpar, or discovering that we just don't have the talent for something we wish we could do well.

Psychologist Steven Hayes has discovered that we will be happier and healthier if we accept that certain things are simply beyond our control. He advises that we stop trying to either change those difficult realities or escape from them and instead focus on what we *can* change—our ways of thinking about them and reacting to them. This is the wisdom expressed by the famous Serenity Prayer, which teaches the power of "the serenity to accept the things I cannot change; courage to change the things I can; and wisdom to know the difference."

Silence

This isn't easy; I know. But here is a simple practice that can be remarkably helpful.

Write down a list of things in your life you wish you could change. Now go through them and reflect on those you can actually change and those you can't. Make a commitment to yourself to stop getting derailed by your emotions about those you can't change and to focus on things you should be doing about those you can. This is a powerful way to motivate yourself to seize the day of the present moment. You'll get better at it the more you build your mindfulness muscles.

Author Jay Dixit explains,

> [Mindfulness] increases the gap between emotional impulse and action, allowing you to do what Buddhists call recognizing the spark before the flame. Focusing on the present reboots your mind so you can respond thoughtfully rather than automatically. Instead of lashing out in anger, backing down in fear, or mindlessly indulging a passing craving, you get the opportunity to say to yourself, "This is the emotion I'm feeling. How should I respond?"[11]

Slow. it. down. Stephen Schueller,[12] a psychologist at the University of Pennsylvania, found that slowing down to take time to appreciate things leads to pleasure. "When subjects in a study took a few minutes each day to actively savor something they usually hurried through—eating a meal, drinking a cup of tea, walking to the bus—they began experiencing more joy, happiness, and other positive emotions, and fewer depressive symptoms," he observed. Think about some things you enjoy doing that you haven't been making much, or any, time for. Make a plan to carve out some time each week to focus only on that activity, bringing all of yourself to it. Deeply engage with all of your senses. Your consciousness of time will fade as you immerse in the moment and you will feel restored.

Go with the flow. The phenomenon of losing our awareness of time is a well-documented component of the experience known as flow. You get into a state of flow when you concentrate on a task so intensely that you become immune to any distractions. Time is not on your mind, and you become entirely one with the moment. You are operating at full power, and the experience is like an adrenaline rush.

In his TED presentation on the subject, "Flow, the Secret to Happiness,"[13] the father of the flow concept, psychologist Mihaly Csikszentmihalyi, recounts the experience of total immersion as a musical composer he interviewed had described it:

Silence

> He doesn't have enough attention left over to monitor how his body feels or his problems at home. He can't feel even that he's hungry or tired, his body disappears, his identity disappears from his consciousness because he doesn't have enough attention, like none of us do, to really do well something that requires a lot of concentration and at the same time to feel that he exists.

In other words, flow involves becoming so mindful of our activity of the moment that we lose all conscious attention to anything else. People who have been in flow have recounted finishing a session of work they had a sense was a couple of hours and discovering that much more time had gone by.

Csikszentmihalyi explains that the defining features of flow are:[14]

- Intense focus and creative engagement.

- A sensation of "ecstasy—of being outside everyday reality."

- Great mental clarity.

- A sense of serenity—no worries about oneself, and a feeling of growing beyond the boundaries of the ego.

- Timelessness—we're thoroughly focused on the present.

- Intrinsic motivation—whatever produces flow becomes its own reward.

Carve out some time to throw yourself into a creative activity you deeply enjoy. It should be something you find challenging but that you can do quite well. That's because one of the conditions for getting into flow is that our skill level is adequate for performing well but that doing so requires intense focus. If the task is too easy, we don't get deeply immersed.

You can start small, though, and work up to more challenging tasks. Csikszentmihalyi notes that engaging in acts of everyday creativity—coloring would be one, and maybe for you, singing or dancing—can give us good hits of what he calls "microflow." This, he says, is "a flow hack, a way of achieving a simulation of rapture but in a relaxed state." Doesn't that sound worth making time for?

Now, let me suggest the mindfulness practice you've probably been expecting. It's the most often promoted practice, and I've saved it for last because I know that many people think it's been hyped, or will think it's old news. I did, too, until I finally tried it and fell in love with it.

A Simple and Brief Meditation

I will be honest. I did not consider meditation as a solution to distraction because I had the wrong idea about what it is and why it is important. I saw the practice as a spiritual endeavor that I didn't need. I also thought it was just the latest flavor of wellness fad, and I was turned off by all the endorsements of celebrities and athletes who promote its benefit in their work, the apps crowding the app stores, and the ubiquitous ads for mindfulness retreats and festivals.

But for this book, I researched it, and I now understand that we can all benefit from practicing some form of meditation. One explanation of why particularly struck me. In an article entitled *The Real Meaning of Meditation*,[15] Swami Rama conveyed the importance of meditation in learning about who we are outside and inside. "From childhood onward, we have been educated only to examine and verify things in the external world. No one has taught us how to look within, to find within, and to verify within. Therefore, we remain strangers to ourselves." Meditation is a way of beginning our journey to look within. In his words,

We remain strangers to ourselves.

> The mind has a mind of its own. Meditation is a practical means for calming yourself, for letting go of your biases and seeing what is, openly and clearly. It is a way of training the mind so that you are not distracted and caught up in its endless churning. You are committing to yourself, to your path, and to the goal of knowing yourself. But at the same time, learning to be calm and still should not become a ceremony or religious ritual; it is a universal requirement of the human body.

There are many resources to help you find a process that works for you. Rama offers the following simple approach,[16] which I am finding is a great help in improving my focus and learning not to indulge in distractions.

Silence

©Dingzeyu Li

He advises:

1. In the yoga tradition, you are guided by a competent teacher to keep your head, neck, and trunk straight while sitting in a meditative posture (asana). When you have learned to be comfortable in this posture, you should form a regular habit of practicing in the same posture at the same time and at the same place every day.

2. Find a simple, uncluttered, quiet place where you will not be disturbed.

3. Sit on the floor with a cushion under you or in a firm chair, with your back straight and your eyes closed.

4. Then bring your awareness slowly down through your body, allowing all of the muscles to relax except those that are supporting your head, neck, and back.

5. Take your time and enjoy the process of letting go of the tension in your body. Meditation is the art and science of letting go, and this letting go begins with the body and then progresses to thoughts.

6. Once the body is relaxed and at peace, bring your awareness to your breath. Notice which part of your body is doing your breathing. If you are breathing primarily with your chest you will not be able to relax. Let your breathing come primarily through the movement of your diaphragm.

7. Continue to observe your breath without trying to control it. At first the breath may be irregular, but gradually it will become smooth.

Chapter 9

8. Allow yourself to experience your breathing in an open and accepting way. Do not judge or attempt to control or change it. Open yourself so fully that eventually there is no distinction between you and the breathing.

9. In this process many thoughts will arise in your mind: Am I doing this right? When will this be over? Perhaps I should have closed the window. I forgot to make an important call. My neck hurts. Hundreds of thoughts may come before you and each thought will call forth some further response: a judgment, an action, an interest in pursuing the thought further, an attempt to get rid of the thought.

10. Bring your attention to these thoughts without reacting to them. You will become aware of how restless your mind is. It tosses and turns like you do on a night when you cannot fall asleep. But if you simply attend to those thoughts when they arise, without reacting, they cannot really disturb you.

11. Remember—it is not the thoughts that disturb you, but your reaction to them.

12. Have patience and do your practice systematically. Every action has a reaction. It is not possible for you to meditate and not receive benefits. You may not notice those benefits now, but slowly and gradually you are storing the samskaras (impressions) in the unconscious mind that will help you later.

13. Be honest with yourself. Keep your mind focused on your goal. It is your own mind that does not allow you to meditate. To work with your mind, you'll have to be patient; you'll have to work with yourself gradually.

Silence

You gain clarity, inner balance, and stability by becoming aware of your inner complexes, biases, immaturities, unproductive reflexes, and habits, according to Swami Rama. "Instead of living in these complexes and habits and acting them out . . . you can give them your full attention," he says. "Only then will they clear."

By genuinely embracing mindfulness, we open up the world both within and around us. We see the world with fresh eyes.

"By acquiring the habit of noticing new things, we recognize that the world is actually changing constantly," says Ellen Jane Langer, professor of psychology at Harvard. The more we understand that, the more we'll appreciate that we have the power within us to change, as well.

Having learned to clear and focus our minds, to tune out all the distraction and reconnect with our authentic values, we're now ready for the next steps of the lifescaling journey—looking deeply within ourselves to discover what we really want to accomplish in our lives and envisioning the path forward.

LIBERATE

Define Success on Your Terms

> "Your time is limited, so don't waste it
> living someone else's life."
> – Steve Jobs

How do you define success? Is it by job title? Income? Assets? Status?

I wrestled mightily with this question and wondered how I should measure success. A mentor long ago asked me, "If you had a choice, would you want to be rich or famous?" The young me quipped, "Why can't I have both?"

I now realize that she was guiding me to think *beyond* both, to my own definition of success. Being rich and famous are crude standards of success that society conditions us to believe will make us happy. She understood that chasing them, seeing them as the purpose of one's work, lures us away from true Happiness.

The understanding of success I learned as a child, which was reinforced throughout my growth into adulthood, was based on the goals and standards taught by my parents, grandparents, teachers, managers, and basically, all other authority figures in my life. It focused too much on a familiar formula:

- Go to church.
- Go to college.
- Work hard and make a good living.
- Make friends.
- Get married.
- Buy a house.
- Buy cars.
- Have children.
- Save money for a rainy day and for retirement.
- Be happy.

It's such a generic prescription, which is so ironic. Many of us are also taught, "You can do anything you set your mind to," encouraged to believe we can achieve almost anything in life. So why has the list of things we *should* achieve been so preordained by all the generations that came before us?

I've been unlearning this wisdom of the ages in order to redefine what success means to me, this time with intent and the understanding that a more mindful, empathetic, loving, and present life is the foundation of success *as a process of living* rather than as a plateau of achievement.

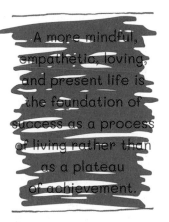

A more mindful, empathetic, loving, and present life is the foundation of success as a process of living rather than as a plateau of achievement.

Success and happiness are mutually exclusive if they're not fundamentally entwined. If we elect to sacrifice happiness for the sake of achieving success, thinking we can focus on being happy later, and that our material success will make us happy, we'll be dearly disappointed.

A plan you have been working on for a long time is beginning to take shape.

©Elena Koycheva

I learned the hard way that success doesn't intrinsically beget happiness. But I also learned that, with mindful attention to what we truly value, our pursuit of happiness can lead to success, which can, in turn, kindle further happiness. They can be powerfully reinforcing, as long as you're defining success on *your* terms.

Ask yourself right now, ~~How do I define success?~~

I spent most of my life chasing someone else's definition of success, checking off accomplishments and pursuing material wealth. Looking in the rearview mirror as I surveyed my life, I realized that I measured my success by how confidently I exuded the message, "Look at me! Look what I've achieved." Maybe that would have made me happy if I hadn't kept raising the bar. But each time I attained a level of achievement I defined as success, it became the new normal, and normal wasn't good enough. I'd find myself pushing for more. The more I had, the more I needed.

It was an exhausting chase because I was seeking satisfaction with my life based on other people's views of me. I was racking up what I thought were trophies of success, which were actually psychological props. I found the most beautiful quotation on the subject. In the words of Nomi Bachar,[1]

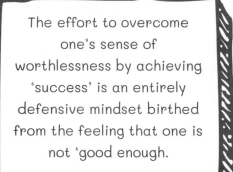

The effort to overcome one's sense of worthlessness by achieving 'success' is an entirely defensive mindset birthed from the feeling that one is not 'good enough.

> The effort to overcome one's sense of worthlessness by achieving 'success' is an entirely defensive mindset birthed from the feeling that one is not 'good enough.' To compensate for that, one must prove their worth through success and notoriety, 'prove it' to doubters of the past, but actually one is trying to 'prove it' to oneself.

I did feel semblances of happiness along the way, in fact, quite often. But, I didn't feel joy or satisfaction. My work on my values and development of a more mindful focus on the potential of the present moment, day after day, allowed me to see that the semblances of happiness I experienced weren't actually fleeting moments of contentment. They were moments of pride, or I should say vanity. I didn't feel gratitude   about my achievements because they didn't matter to me intrinsically; their value rested entirely too much in their social currency.

Meanwhile all of the stuff I accumulated, mostly so that I could show I had it, started to weigh on me. I learned that with stuff comes pressure to maintain and use it. Otherwise, stuff sits there and becomes a taunting reminder of all the work we've done to get it, and how little time we have to enjoy it. So much of our stuff becomes emotional baggage. Not only does it fail to give us joy, it constantly pulls at our subconscious because we know it is coming at such a cost. We look at it and calculate the opportunity costs in lost family and friend time, lost restorative leisure time, and lost sense of what would actually fulfill us.

Not all of our stuff is burdensome. There's nothing wrong with wanting stuff if we authentically want it, because having it is meaningful to us. Buying an expensive painting is great to do if the work feeds your soul, or you want to foster an artist's career, or assure the painting is well cared for. If you don't stop to look at it sometimes, and feel the meaning to you of its presence, then it has lost its true value.

Some of the stuff we chase reminds us of good times we've had, of steps achieved, of passions we've cherished, like my old guitars. They were good baggage, and I'm so glad I didn't get rid of them because they're now giving me so much joy again. Some of our stuff embodies aspects of who we are.

In order to release yourself from your burdensome baggage, you've got to unpack all of your baggage and take a good look at what you're really carrying around with you.

All You Need Is Less.

@briansolis

This is a pivotal moment in lifescaling. We need to decide what we are taking with us, what we need for the journey forward, and what we should leave behind.

I'll never forget the deep emotional impact of reading a quote by Thich Nhat Hanh,[2] Vietnamese Buddhist monk and peace activist, which has stayed with me: "Letting go gives us freedom and freedom is the only condition for happiness." It was 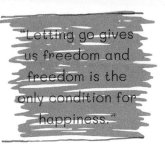 one of those right time, right place messages, and it immediately changed my outlook on *stuff*. Suddenly, I could see that I was tethered to lots of stuff that was nothing but emotional clutter. It didn't mean anything to me, and I don't think it really impressed anyone else, either.

Learning how to shed the weight of tokens of success is the next step of lifescaling. Here's what to do:

Step 1: Take an inventory of your baggage and assess it by thinking about why you wanted it, what it meant to you when you got it, and what it means to you now. This goes not only for material possessions, but for all the indicators of your success—the good grades you strived for, the promotions you gunned for and new jobs secured, the trips taken, concerts attended, dinners with friends, and holidays with family. You get the drill.

Step 2: Mentally gather up the stuff that's become emotional baggage. Keep in mind as you do this that not all of the emotional weight we feel is negative. Some of it is the product of the healthy pursuit of dreams. For example, if you have an extensive to-do list of ambitious goals, you're probably feeling some guilt or frustration that you're not getting to them quickly enough.

In my case, I have so many things I want to create—a musical album, three different books, several research reports on topics I would love to cover, and a touring pop-up shop for my photography and art. These are all projects that are truly meaningful to me. But I've learned that I need to set some of them aside for a while in order to maintain my creative focus. I just can't get to everything, and taking my desire to start working on *all* of them with me everywhere was limiting my ability to create *any* of them.

Other elements of my exhausting baggage were the stuff I thought attested to my success from which I took no true satisfaction. I had to sort through everything carefully, really challenging myself to admit what it meant to me, in order to see which was which clearly.

Step 3: Give yourself permission to let go of the things that are holding you back, not only those you don't really want but also your aspirations that are positive and worthy of creation. Plan to revisit them later. Put them away for safekeeping.

With those material things you've decided are just weighing on you, think about giving them away. You could take them to Goodwill. Or maybe sell them on eBay. Consider all new purchases you're planning carefully to be honest with yourself about why you want those things. Do you really need the newest iPhone? Could you happily get a few more good years out of your current car?

With your false trappings of success offloaded, you're now free to begin redefining what success means to you.

As I worked on that, by good fortune, I came across a commencement speech by the actor Matthew McConaughey.[3] By any measure, he is one of the most successful actors of his generation. What he had to say about success resonated deeply with me, and it resonates with the theme of this chapter.

He presented a challenge to the graduating students:

Liberate

The question that we've got to ask ourselves is, what success is to us and what success is to you.

> Is it more money?

> Maybe it's a healthy family.

> Maybe it's a happy marriage.

> Maybe it's to help others.

> Maybe it's to be famous.

> . . . to be spiritually sound?

> . . . to leave the world a little bit of a better place than you found it.

Continue to ask yourself that question. Your answer may change over time and that's fine. But, do yourself this favor. Whatever your answer is, don't choose anything that will jeopardize your soul. Prioritize who you are and who you want to be, and don't spend time with anything that antagonizes your character.

Be brave. Take the hill. But first, answer that question, what's my hill?

. . .

Be discerning. Choose it because you want it. Choose it because you want to. We're going to make mistakes. You've got to own them. Then you've got to make amends. And then you've got to move on.

You are the author of the book of your life.

> You can live mindlessly as you follow worn scripts for success and react to life. Or you can define your own standards of success.

We're all on this planet for an undefined amount of time (at least that I know of). While you're here, you can live life according to the standards, expectations, and beliefs of others. You can live mindlessly as you follow worn scripts for success and react to life. Or you can define your own standards of success.

Let go of the milestones set out for you by earlier generations.

Their life's pursuit, their materialistic possessions, their life status . . . is . . . theirs . . . not yours.

Get comfortable with wanting something different.

You and only you can live your truth (although others will try).

The way to do that with authenticity is to gain clarity about your life's purpose, for this stage of your journey.

Finding life purpose is a profoundly personal, mindful, and soulful process. It requires answering the question, *What can I do with my time that is mindful, important, and meaningful, to give the gift of creativity, love, knowledge, peace, and joy to others and myself?*

In the chapters ahead, I will lead you through the powerful set of methods I used to answer that question.

PURPOSE

The Purpose
of Life Is
Purposeful Living

> "Nothing we ever imagined is beyond our powers,
> only beyond our present self-knowledge."
> – Theodore Roszak

———————————

I believe you can find the person in you who can inspire you to pursue the goals that are most meaningful to you, no matter what others may think of them, or how far away they may seem.

It is time you believe this about you, too.

We can always find lots of reasons, and other people, to blame for why we're where we are in life versus where we want to be.

Do not allow excuse-making to hold you back any longer.

Your dreams are too precious to give anyone or anything the power to keep you from them, including you.

Stop doubting. Stop thinking about all the reasons why not. Break the cycle.

From here on out, it's on *you* to make change happen.

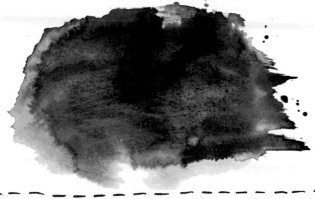

Harder than making change is recognizing and accepting our need for it. Doing so requires us to acknowledge that so much of what we've been doing has gotten us off course. Deep down, we know that there are ways in which we have not been helping ourselves, or have even been shooting ourselves in the foot. But we silence that voice of awareness. We convince ourselves that we've been making investments in getting to where we want to go, and that the lessons we've learned, the pain we've endured, the milestones of highs and lows we've experienced have been in the service of self-betterment and personal growth. But without aim and objectives, without intention, those investments, life experiences, and pivotal moments may not steer us in the most meaningful direction. "If you don't know where you are going, then any road will get you there," wrote Lewis Carroll,[1] author of *Alice's Adventure in Wonderland and Through the Looking-Glass.*

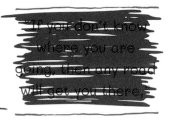

©Rye Jessen

A wonderful article[2] on life purpose by Hélène Tragos Stelian described how so many of us meander through life versus taking intentional acts toward specific outcomes. She wrote, "I have lived most of my life 'mindlessly,' that is, without clear thought behind my actions and decisions. I chose the college I did because that's where my older brother was going, joined a sorority because that's what 'everybody' was doing, majored in History because it had few credit requirements, pursued a career in retailing for lack of any other interests, married my first husband because I was afraid of being alone—you get the picture."

Stelian then shared that she'd had a life-changing realization when she turned 50. "I finally had a wake-up call that, with several decades of empty-nesting ahead of me, it wasn't too late: I could still craft a more 'conscious' life for myself." That's when she decided to choose what her future should look like and then live life in that direction. She combined her interests in human connection, psychology, research, writing, and teaching, along with her dedication to performance and results, and identified her strengths, passions, and values to craft a mission statement for her life.

> My personal mission is to use my talent for researching and synthesizing ideas, along with my passion for informing others, to challenge, empower, and inspire people to purposeful and transformative action.

Now, as an executive leadership consultant, her mission statement serves as her *guiding star*. Because she has articulated it, it provides her with clear direction whenever she comes to a decision point in her life. She wakes up every day knowing why she's on this planet and what she's meant to do, excited for the journey ahead.

Take a moment. I'm going to ask you a question and I want you to be ready to reflect on it. You don't need to answer it fully yet; you're probably not ready to respond. That's just fine. Just let it roll around in your mind as you keep reading.

~~What is the reason you live?~~

I had thought I knew the answer to that question. But as I dove into the work for this book, I realized I just had semblances of purpose in my life mixed in with realities of responsibility. I was confusing the two as I tried to function as best I could. That was in part because I'd never really been asked to articulate what my purpose in life was, or what I wanted it to be. I'd been *told* lots of things about what it was—to be a good student, to make a good salary, to be a good parent. But I had not been encouraged to delve deeply into my personal values and aspirations to find my purpose. In fact, I'd been led to think that purpose is *out there* and will come to us.

Don't Chase Purpose *Out There;*
Look Within to Appreciate Who You Are
and Discover Who You Are Not

I don't know about you, but I was told by my parents, and learned from books, movies, and TV shows, that to find a sense of purpose we have to venture out in the world and search for it. That notion has appeal because it suggests life is an adventure in which we'll eventually discover what we're meant to be doing, often entirely by chance. It doesn't require us to do the work of grappling with setting our own course; it suggests we'll find our way to a life rich in purpose by following the basic recipe of success and a flash of serendipity.

That can certainly happen, but let me ask you, how long do you want to wait for that lightening to strike?

> How long do you want to wait for that lightening to strike?

Did you know that the average life expectancy for Americans is 78.7 years?[3] That means living to witness 28,725 sunrises or sunsets (whichever motivates you more). Multiply your age by 365 and subtract that number from 28,725. That's how many (estimated, of course) sunsets or sunrises you have in the time gifted to you to make an impact, to do something with your life that you love, to become the person you aspire to be.

Purpose

This is one of those humbling and maybe even upsetting thought exercises. Yet, it's so helpful in sparking motivation to get going with the things you really want your days to be about. Do you want to be one of those people who on their deathbed are regretting all of the *could have*, *should have*, *would have*, *wish I had*s they didn't do?

Alright. Alright. Alright. Take Charge of Defining Your Own Sense of Purpose

In the 1993 coming of age film *Dazed and Confused*, the one that launched Matthew McConaughey's career, his character, David Wooderson, uttered this line that would become his catchphrase and part of the modern vernacular, "Alright. Alright. Alright." Those now iconic words, his first lines ever on film, were completely unscripted.

The origin story of "Alright. Alright. Alright." is pretty cool. McConaughey shared what happened behind the scenes, before shooting that now famous scene, in a 2011 interview.[4]

"So we go up to the set. I get in the car 'cause I'm nervous. First scene ever on film. And right before we're about to shoot I've got friends in the car and I had been listening to this live Doors album and in between two of the songs Morrison goes, 'Alright! Alright! Alright! Alright!'

'Alright! Alright! Alright! Alright!'"

> "So right before we're about to go, I go, 'What is Wooderson about? He's about four things: He's about his car, he's about gettin' high, he's about rock 'n' roll and pickin' up chicks.' I go, 'I'm in my car, I'm high as a kite, I'm listenin' to rock 'n' roll...' Action ... and there's the chick. 'Alright, alright, alright ...' three out of four!"

McConaughey wasn't just following the movie's script and taking direction. Right from his very first scene in his first movie he was applying his creativity to being self-directed. He was not only shaping that fictional character, he was shaping his own future, from the very beginning working to give the kind of inspired and distinctive performance that has made his acting so captivating. That creative approach led to his Best Actor win at the 86th Academy Awards for his performance in *Dallas Buyers Club*. And he didn't rest his laurels following that win. He's continued to craft mesmerizing performances, such as in Christopher Nolan's *Interstellar* and Martin Scorsese's *The Wolf of Wall Street*.

He's not only talented; he's focused and driven by a purpose to achieve true artistry.

Right here, right now, choose to define and pursue a life of purpose according to *your* values.

Purpose

©rawpixel

Discovering the Purpose of Purpose

According to the Oxford Dictionary, purpose is *the reason* for which something is done or created or for which something exists. That's probably the sense of the word most of us begin with, but a *life purpose* is so much more. Purpose is not just the rationale for doing or creating something; it is the lifeforce that keeps you energized and motivated. It fosters physical, mental, and spiritual strength. Purpose is what separates mediocrity from greatness. It gets you out of bed each day with the fire and determination to create something incredible or perform some amazing feat showcasing your brilliant mind and bright soul. It's mindful and deeply personal, and it must be articulated.

According to Steve Taylor, PhD, senior lecturer in psychology at Leeds Metropolitan University in the UK, and author of *The Leap: The Psychology of Spiritual Awakening*, says "Purpose is a fundamental component of a fulfilling life."[5]

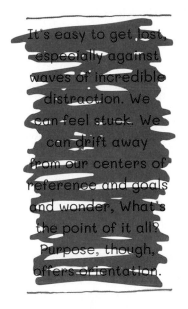
It's easy to get lost, especially against waves of incredible distraction. We can feel stuck. We can drift away from our centers of reference and goals and wonder, What's the point of it all? Purpose, though, offers orientation.

It's easy to get lost, especially against waves of incredible distraction. We can feel stuck. We can drift away from our centers of reference and goals and wonder, *What's the point of it all*? Purpose, though, offers orientation.[6]

Why does purpose have such positive effects?[7] For one thing, research has shown that a clear sense of purpose makes us less vulnerable to what Taylor calls "psychological discord." This is the sense of unease we experience whenever our attention isn't engaged. It makes us susceptible to distraction, which we've seen fosters negative and unproductive feelings and behaviors. It can also manifest into anxiety and depression. Clarity of purpose helps us focus our mental energy on positive and productive activities.

Clarity of purpose helps us focus our mental energy on positive and productive activities.

Purpose is also good for our psychological health because it enhances our self-esteem. When we avert distraction and focus in order to create and achieve our goals, we feel capable and successful.

Purpose also pulls us out of our harmful self-focus and makes us feel part of something bigger, beyond ourselves. It frees us from our rumination about ourselves and the past and keeps us oriented toward the future, with a sense of what we can contribute. That fuels our creativity.

According to researchers Jorunn Drageset, Gorill Haugan, and Oscar Tranvåg,[8] there are four main experiences that foster a strong sense of purpose in life:

©Austin Chan

1. **Physical and mental well-being:** Taking care of your body, health, mind, and soul.

2. **Belonging and recognition:** Feeling valued and validated and valuing and validating those who are important to you.

3. **Personally treasured activities:** Populating our days, consistently, with the things that make us feel authentically happy.

4. **Spiritual closeness and connectedness:** Spirituality is not necessarily tied to belief in a religion, or even in any sort of god. It is a feeling of being part of a collective experience that transcends ourselves and encompasses humanity as a whole.[9] In his article "Spirituality as Connectedness,"[10] author Richard Hill writes that spiritual practice "encompasses the activities engaged in by people to enable conscious awareness of connection and to enhance the experience of the connective process, leading to even deeper levels of interaction and integration." That mindful sense of how connected we are, with our family and friends, our communities, and truly with all other living beings on the planet, helps us appreciate how important our contribution can be to so many lives.

Purpose Is Your North Star

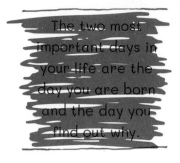

The two most important days in your life are the day you are born and the day you find out why.

To live purposefully is an ongoing journey. It is said that the two most important days in your life are the day you are born and the day you find out why.[11] I love that, but I'd change the *why* to *what for*. I'd also add that discovering your *what for* is not a one-time event. The way you define your purpose will continue to evolve.

When Matthew McConaughey won the Oscar in 2014, in his acceptance speech, he cited three things he needs each day:

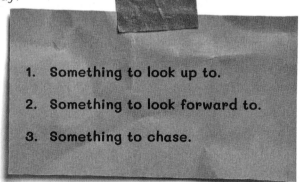

1. Something to look up to.

2. Something to look forward to.

3. Something to chase.

First, McConaughey said he looked up to God who has graced his life with opportunities.

Second, he looked forward to his family—who's always there for him, always supporting him.

Third, he said he chases his hero.

Who's his hero?

McConaughey said that when he was 15, someone asked him who his hero was, and after thinking about it for some time he said, "I know who my hero is—it's me in 10 years."

Ten years later when McConaughey turned 25, the same person asked him, "So, are you a hero?"

He said he was not even close. "Every day, every week, every month, and every year of my life, my hero is always 10 years away," he said. "I'm never going to be my hero. I'm not going to obtain that; I know I'm not, and that's just fine with me because that keeps me with somebody to keep on chasing."

Living purposefully is to live in a state of constant growth. But because life is such a juggling act, to set our course and to stay true to our purpose as we continue to evolve, we need a point of reference we can always rely on—a North Star. This is where writing out a purpose helps. It assists, on a daily basis, with deciding how to spend our time.

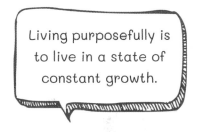

Living purposefully is to live in a state of constant growth.

So, let's get you started crafting your own mission statement for this leg of your lifescaling journey, which I will call your purpose statement.

The Purpose of Life Questions

Grab a piece of paper or open a new note or document on your laptop, tablet, or phone.

Please write out the following questions[1] and do your best to dig deep and answer them:

1. What was I most passionate about as a child or young adult?

2. What do I dream of becoming now?

3. What do I feel I am missing in my life today? (What feelings are absent, what achievements or goals unaccomplished?)

4. Be honest with yourself, ask why you really want to change?

5. What are the reasons you feel this change is positive for you?

6. What are the habits you do every day that are preventing you from making the change you want to happen?

Note: From this point on, as the questions get a little more challenging, I have added my own answers to help spur your thoughts.

7. How would you like to grow? What does it take for you to manifest this change?

8. How do I want to feel every day? (Beyond the easy answers, that is, happy, fulfilled, successful, and so on)

   My responses included:

   - I want to feel the freedom and have the permission to create, to be creative, to experiment out loud.
   - I want to feel inspired, energized, and that I'm always growing.
   - I want to feel like I'm creating value in this world and that I'm leaving it in a better place than it would be without me.
   - I want to feel contentment, pleasure, and satisfaction with my current accomplishments.

9. What things can I do every day that put me on a path to those feelings?

   My responses included:

   - I want a career and hobbies that allow me to be creative in all I do.
   - I would like to start getting out again, surround myself with people I admire as well as those I need to know.
   - I want my work to impact the lives of others to help them learn, unlearn, and grow.
   - I want to take pause regularly to enjoy what I've done, learned, and earned thus far.

Purpose

10. What work can I do that lets me pursue these activities? How can I make a living that keeps me feeling like this?

My thoughts:

- I will focus on the three creative aspects of my professional life that give me a feeling of having value, that bring me happiness, and that allow me to positively impact others: (1) speaking, (2) content creation, (3) authorship. I will formally commit, and give myself space, to embrace artistic hobbies where I can express creativity regardless of ROI.

- I will find events to attend, like I used to, where like-minded souls who are well on their journey or constantly exploring how to be their best selves and how to make the greatest impact on our world are in attendance. I will attend and host dinners and intellectual salons with friends, role models, and others who inspire me—even if I don't know them yet.

- I will take more time with immediate family and my best friends to celebrate life. I will be thankful for what we have and take time to remind everyone and everything how much I appreciate them in my life.

- Everything that doesn't add to or that takes away from this will be removed from my life.

This exercise is a great route to awakening. I hope you are now buzzing with inspiration about the changes in your life you want to begin making. When I did it, this exercise made me feel hopeful and driven; it also made me feel disbelief. I was dumbfounded that I hadn't yet gone through this exercise in my life.

Articulate and Picture a Life Worth Living: State Your Purpose and Identify Your Purpose Pillars

Now you want to draw on your answers to those questions, as well as reflect on the set of leading values you identified earlier, and write a declarative statement that summarizes the life purpose to which you are committing. It can be a sentence or two or it can be longer, as I'll show you in a bit. I found writing mine challenging, so I researched purpose statements to find some solid examples to share with you. In doing so, I discovered great ones from a few of my idols.[12] I knew there was a reason I was drawn to them!

Purpose

Oprah Winfrey

"To be a teacher. And to be known for inspiring my students to be more than they thought they could be."

In an issue of O magazine, Winfrey recalls watching her grandmother churn butter and wash clothes in a cast-iron pot in the yard. A small voice inside told her that her life would be more than hanging clothes on a line. She realized she wanted to be a teacher, but "I never imagined it would be on TV," she writes.

Sir Richard Branson

"To have fun in [my] journey through life and learn from [my] mistakes. In business, know how to be a good leader and always try to bring out the best in people. It's very simple: listen to them, trust in them, believe in them, respect them, and let them have a go!"[13]

Branson has Sir Richard Branson's sentiment was shared in an interview with Motivated magazine. His unconventional leadership approach has earned him cult-like status. According to Forbes, he is now worth over 5 billion US dollars.

Amanda Sternberg, founder of Dailyworth.com

"To use my gifts of intelligence, charisma, and serial optimism to cultivate the self-worth and net-worth of women around the world."

Steinberg launched DailyWorth in 2009, to help women build wealth because she believes, "Financially empowered women are the key to world peace." The site has since blossomed to more than one million subscribers.

In further researching best-in-class examples, I found an incredible resource in author Susan D. Kalior's work. Trained as a psychotherapist, she has gone on to write many books and offer workshops about how to live a creative, purposeful, and fulfilling life. Her website is www.manifestyourpotential.com. She offers a pair of before and after purpose statements that show how to give a statement clarity and specificity. The first is too vague while the second has great, actionable detail.

Before:

I Have Always Wanted To . . .

I have always wanted to do something about . . . saving wildlife. When I was growing up, I watched all the nature shows and poured over *National Geographic* magazine for hours. I love being around animals so for a while I thought I wanted to work in a zoo. I also thought about being a . . . chef, but decided it wasn't right for me. My best subject in school was writing, so I got a college degree in English and now I am working in an advertising firm.

After:

My Life Purpose Is . . .

I want to be a spokesman for wildlife issues and help people connect their daily actions to saving the wildlife on this planet.

Using my warm, engaging voice to create animal voices over the camp stove and after dinner over the campfire, I will share stories that highlight the wonders of the natural world and our connection with the animals and wildlife with whom we share this planet. Finding the humor in daily situations, I will transform the safari and wildlife outback camping trip into an adventure that opens and changes hearts—and starts a wave of quiet understanding and activism for saving endangered species and supporting sustainable environments for wildlife.

After building up a loyal client base, lots of connections with kindred spirits, and an awesome network, when I am ready to settle down, I will take my collection of campfire tested and refined stories and record them, becoming a spokesman for endangered species.

The differences are in vision, specificity, and the basis for accountability.

Now, let me show you how I took my answers to the Purpose of Life Questions and my values work and drew on them to write my purpose statement.

As a reminder, here is where I ended in the Purpose for Lifescaling exercise:

I will focus on the three creative aspects of my professional life where I feel value, happiness, and impact: (1) speaking, (2) content creation, (3) authorship. I will formally commit, and give myself space to embrace artistic hobbies where I can express creativity regardless of financial ROI.

I will find events to attend, like I used to, where like-minded souls who are well on their journey or constantly exploring how to be their best selves and how to make the greatest impact on our world, are in attendance. I will attend and host dinners and intellectual salons with friends, role models, and others who inspire me—even if I don't know them yet.

I will take more time with immediate family and my best friends to celebrate life. I will be thankful for what we have and take time to remind everyone and everything how much I appreciate them in my life.

Everything that doesn't add to or that takes away from this will be removed from my life.

I distilled those commitments into this statement:

I aim to be a creative and inspiring author, speaker, and content creator who focuses on helping people understand how technology and human behavior is evolving and how that is affecting business, markets, communities, and personal lives.

Through my work, I aim to create opportunities for people that I did not have personally and professionally. I will seek to know who they are, their challenges, and share insight through content of all forms to guide them toward new opportunities.

To connect the dots, I will use my networks to connect with people who can help me help others, who will challenge and inspire me, and who will link me to others who can raise the caliber and scale the reach of my work.

To get there, I will also focus on me . . .

- The relationships that are important to where I am and where I need to be

- My mental (intellectual quotient or IQ), physical (PQ), emotional (EQ), and spiritual (SQ) health and awareness

- My capacity (means) to care for myself and my loved ones and give them the opportunities to explore their life purpose over time

- My ability to feel empathy, sympathy, and gratitude to live happily, respectfully, thankfully, and with dignity

From Purpose Statement to Pillars of Purpose

I am a visual thinker, and I have found creating images that encapsulate information I've learned very helpful in keeping a reminder handy that I can quickly consult regularly. So, I decided to create a graphic to represent what I call the pillars of my newly purpose-driven life. They form the foundation on which I will build as I continue to pursue and evolve my purpose. You may want to create your own version. To do so, first think about the set of main commitments you are making for your new life. Here are the ones I listed, and the way I represented them.

My Pillars of Purpose

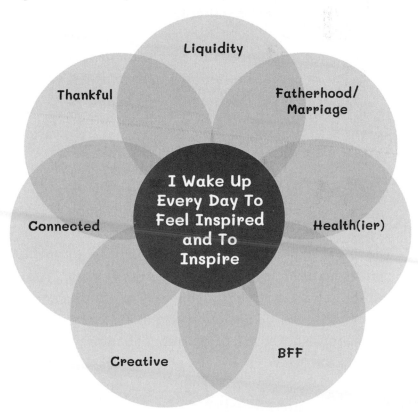

1. Liquidity: I aim to support my family and loved ones and have reasonable choices and flexibility for life's important moments, stages, and events. Also, I seek, and I've learned the hard way, to facilitate family time in everyday routines and also excursions that break us from those routines so that we can grow together.

2. Fatherhood and Marriage: I will live life so that as I learn, my family learns and as they learn, I learn. I will be an active listener, a strong and loving leader (partner), a guiding light, an approachable teacher, an empathetic and compassionate friend, consistent role model, and a present, loving, fun, and nurturing father/husband/brother/son/uncle/cousin/nephew. In marriage, I will ask the same. No relationship is a one-way street.

3. Health(ier): I will love my mind, body, and spirit and live a healthier lifestyle; eat more consciously; exercise regularly; practice focus, mindfulness, presence, and depth; constantly learn and unlearn; establish positive and productive routines and nourishing behaviors; and surround myself with like-minded and aspirational friends, colleagues, and role-models. I will also free myself of stuff and emotional baggage that is weighing me down.

4. BFF: There are several people in my life to which I will dedicate time to cultivate more meaningful relationships. There are also people I've not yet met, but need to, and I will open my closed doors to new friendships. There are certain people in my life (and I'm sure there will be others) who lead me astray, sap precious energy, and leave me feeling worse about myself.

5. Creative: I will hone my artistry and practice creativity in all I do, from everyday work to fantastical creations. I will explore more creative and productive outlets beyond those I use to make a living, to stay sharp, improve my skills and capabilities, and give my permission to enjoy (not stress over) my expressions to feel happiness during the process of creating and in my output.

6. Connected: I will plug into the communities where I can continue to learn and be inspired. I will also connect to the communities where my creativity can benefit others directly, create new opportunities for those who seek it, and do so at scale.

Purpose

7. Thankful: I will slow down to appreciate my blessings, all of the wonderful people in my life, the experiences (big and small), the work I'm fortunate enough to create (day in and day out), the cherished things I've earned over the years, my health and the time I've had and have right now. Gratitude reciprocates.

I'm committing to hold all seven in a loving and nurturing heart and a dedicated embrace. Investing in each pillar of purpose takes daily work and this is why we must choose carefully the goals to which we're committing. Too many pillars of purpose mean you will have spread yourself too thin to succeed. Too few give you room to develop and grow and build new pillars as needed.

Keep in mind always that you are going to make missteps. You'll falter, encounter failures, and doubt yourself along the way. We all do.

Remember, living purposefully is an ongoing process, not a one-and-done achievement. A positive outlook is vital to keeping your energy up and motivation strong. So, let's next take a good look at how we cultivate a positive mindset.

ENERGIZE

Positivity Opens
the Doors to
Our Destinations

Now that you've defined the what for you want to refocus your time and energy on, let's consider the how of dedicating yourself to the daily pursuit of those life-regenerating goals. I've already revealed that I'm a Disney geek. One of my favorite Disney movies is the classic Pinocchio. Every time I watch it, I still choke up a little at the song When You Wish Upon a Star. To this day, it inspires me. It reminds me to imagine. It encourages me to believe.

Without singing the song to you, the essence of it, what really matters, is that to open doors of possibility and opportunity, do more than "wish" upon a star. Instead, dream. Be a dreamer. And, believe in your dream and believe in yourself. Let your imagination define you. Most importantly, transcend the acts of wishing upon a star. Anyone can do that. It's those whose dreams and imagination become so vivid on the inside that they influence the outside world around them and reshape their destiny and those whom they touch.

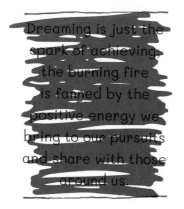

Dreaming is just the spark of achieving; the burning fire is fanned by the positive energy we bring to our pursuits and share with those around us.

I absolutely love the message of believing in our power to fulfill our dreams, and especially the emphasis on the importance of our hearts being in them. That's another way of saying they are our authentic, self-determined aspirations. I also love the notion that good things can come to us unexpectedly, and that the world is not out to get us; that there is a force of good operating in the universe. But it's more than just having hope. I also believe that we must not rely on wishing and believing in fate as the route to achieving our dreams. Once you have a dream, shape it, stoke it, bring it to life and let it flourish. This is your power. This is your gift.

Dreaming is just the spark of achieving; the burning fire is fanned by the positive energy we bring to our pursuits and share with those around us.

I readily admit that I am no an expert about how the universe works, but I do believe in the power of positive thinking. You've probably heard some form of a popular quote, often credited to Henry Ford, that goes something like this: *If you think you can or if you think you can't, you're right.*[1]

©Javardh

The message that the way we think is the key determinant of our success was popularized by Wallace Wattles in his 1910 book, *The Science of Getting Rich*.[2] He famously wrote:

> THOUGHT is the only power which can produce tangible riches from the Formless Substance. The stuff from which all things are made is a substance which thinks, and a thought of form in this substance produces the form.

For a book that's over 100 years old, it continues to have a profound effect on society, in part through more recent motivational writers like Tony Robbins, author of *Awaken the Giant Within*, and Rhonda Byrne, author of *The Secret*.

The essence of what these modern motivators share can still be found in Wattles' words, "A man's way of doing things is the direct result of the way he thinks about things."

Of course, we've all heard the advice that we should think positively, but it's a whole lot easier said than done. And that's in part because we know we can't just think outcomes into being. That's how the power of positive thinking is sometimes portrayed, and we rightfully roll our eyes. Wattles himself stressed the *doing* that our thinking influences, and that part of his message has sometimes been overlooked.

We may also push back about thinking positively because we see ourselves as realists, and after all, lots of bad things happen in the world, and to us and our loved ones. Our minds also naturally put more emphasis on bad than good.

Psychologists and neurobiologists have found that a negativity bias is hardwired into our brains. We remember negative experiences, and the negative aspects of experiences that are a combination of good and bad, more vividly. Whatever unpleasant thoughts, emotions, and difficult sensations are involved in an experience—such as if we overstrain a muscle during a workout that was otherwise wonderfully energizing—have a greater and lasting effect on our psychological state than neutral or positive experiences.[3]

©Kyle Glenn

Why is this? One idea is that reacting more strongly to things that hurt us was good for our survival. This is backed up by the fact that we react to negative stimuli faster.[4] An intensity of focus on and quick reaction to threats was important when we lived out on the open savanna surrounded by wild animals. But in modern life, it can blind us to good things happening and opportunities we can seize. That not only means we miss lots of opportunities; it can also lead us to adopt a generally pessimistic view of life and construct a dispiriting story of the nature of our lives.

Nobel Prize winning psychologist Daniel Kahneman explained this in his 2010 TED Talk,[5] "The Riddle of Experience versus Memory."

"There is an 'experiencing self' who lives in the present and who knows the present. And then there's 'the remembering self,' the person who keeps score and maintains the story of our lives," he says.

How we feel about the experiences we have in the moment and how we remember the experiences are very different, with only about a 50 percent correlation. Kahneman illustrates this point with the story of a man who experienced a "glorious" performance of a symphony. At the end of the performance, this person quite emotionally recalled one moment of a "dreadful screeching sound," that "ruined the whole experience." Kahneman points out that it was really only the memory of the experience that was ruined. "He had the experience. He had 20 minutes of glorious music. They counted for nothing."

This is another reason that training our minds to focus on the present moment is so important—it allows us to see the good along with the bad.

Training our minds to focus on the present moment is so important—it allows us to see the good along with the bad.

Positivity Does Not Mean Denial

A common criticism of the advice to cultivate positive thinking is that it encourages us to turn a blind eye to problems and to deny our pain, frustration, or anger. This is an unfortunate misunderstanding. The explanation of a positive mindset on the website[6] for Martin Seligman's Positive Psychology Program at the University of Pennsylvania clarifies that positive thinking

... is not about being constantly happy or cheerful, and it's not about ignoring anything negative or unpleasant in your life. It's about incorporating both the positive and negative into your perspective and choosing to still be generally optimistic.

It's about acknowledging that you will not always be happy and learning to accept bad moods and difficult emotions when they come.

Above all, it's about increasing your control over your own attitude in the face of whatever comes your way. You cannot control your mood, and you cannot always control the thoughts that pop into your head, but you can choose how you handle them.

> You cannot control your mood, and you cannot always control the thoughts that pop into your head, but you can choose how you handle them.

The site also points out the incredibly wide-ranging benefits of cultivating positivity. A highly selective list includes that positive thinking:

- increases productivity

- decreases burnout

- leads to better assessments of us by our employers

- increases creativity

- improves our overall psychological well-being

It's also great for our physical health. The site reports that,

> According to the experts at the Mayo Clinic, positive thinking can increase your lifespan, reduce rates of depression and levels of distress, give you greater resistance to the common cold . . . improve your cardiovascular health and protect you from cardiovascular disease.

How can we not want to be more positive!

Stanford Professor Carol Dweck[7] has studied the role of one's mindset in success. She distinguishes between a "fixed mindset" and a "growth mindset."[8] Individuals with fixed mindsets, she explains, view their skills as constant personal traits and they tend to take setbacks hard and to judge themselves harshly, whereas people with growth mindsets view their skills as malleable abilities that can be improved.

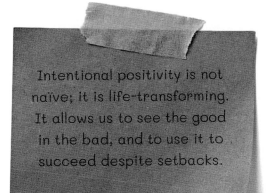

Intentional positivity is not naïve; it is life-transforming. It allows us to see the good in the bad, and to use it to succeed despite setbacks.

We want to cultivate a positive growth mindset. That will allow us to pursue our purpose with passionate energy. Intentional positivity is not naïve; it is life-transforming. It allows us to see the good in the bad, and to use it to succeed despite setbacks.

We might tend to think that we are just born with a certain temperament, that we're either a natural optimist or are a pessimist, and there's not much we can do if we're a pessimist. But brain science has shown otherwise. We can learn not to close our eyes to opportunity. Yes, the negativity bias is built into our brains, but we can teach our brains to override it. We can cultivate a positive mindset. We can actually modify our brains.

Growing a New Brain

In his 1890 book *The Principles of Psychology*, Harvard psychologist William James wrote, "In most of us, by the age of thirty, the character has set like plaster, and will never soften again." This is believed to be the first statement in modern psychology that one's personality becomes fixed at a particular point in life.[9] That belief held sway for decades.

But a host of more recent research has shown that our brains are not, in fact, just fixed at some point. They are constantly changing, and we can, to some degree, guide how they change by how we think.

"Thought changes structure," observed psychiatrist Norman Doidge,[10] in his book *The Brain that Changes Itself*. The more you train your brain, the more you reshape it. Essentially, the brain is capable of re-engineering and we are the engineers.

To take good advantage of this *plasticity* of the brain, as it's called, we have to direct our thoughts with intention. Otherwise, we'll just fall back into ruts of automatic thinking.

As Deborah Ancona, a professor of management and organizational studies at MIT, shared in an interview,[11] "We . . . develop neural pathways, and the more we use those neural pathways over years and years and years, they become very stuck and deeply embedded, moving into deeper portions of the brain." Those established thought patterns make it "hard to break free of them." Tara Swart, a senior lecturer at MIT, illuminated why we do so in her book *Neuroscience for Leadership*:[12] "Our brain is 'inherently lazy' and will always 'choose the most energy efficient path if we let it.'" The established path is the easy route.

Energize

©Greg Rakozy

Over time, our neural programming creates a series of mental models that help us navigate our lives. The clearest explanation of them I found comes from entrepreneur and author James Clear:[13]"Mental models guide your perception and behavior. They are the thinking tools that you use to understand life, make decisions, and solve problems."

They can be hugely helpful, allowing us to make quick decisions in circumstances that are familiar, for example. But if we let them, they will essentially dictate how we think about and react to people, things, and events. For instance, my immediate eye-rolling reaction to the description of Dr. Rao as a happiness guru resulted from a model I'd constructed that suggested I should be cynical about any such characterizations. That was because I had read so much unfounded and misleading writing by people hyped as gurus. It was only because I was researching this book, and his TED talk had been highly recommended, that I went ahead and watched it.

> "Learning a new mental model gives you a new way to see the world."

We can't stop our brains from constructing these ways of thinking, but thankfully, we can train them to construct new ones, which unlocks new vistas of possibility. As James Clear notes, "Learning a new mental model gives you a new way to see the world." Research has proven that with conscious effort to retrain our brains, we can accomplish amazing changes.

We can increase our intelligence (IQ).

We can become more emotionally intelligent.

We can recover from certain types of brain damage.

We can unlearn destructive or unproductive behaviors, values, and habits.

We can also make positive thinking a mindset.

Martin Seligman's Positive Psychology program site offers a wealth of suggestions for ways to do this, and I encourage you to consult it. Here, I'll just offer a few of the methods that I've found most helpful and enjoyable.

 **Make a list of everything you're thankful or grateful for.**[14] Take a moment and think about everything in your life today or the experiences, people, or things that have helped you. This is such a simple exercise, but it has a profound effect on your outlook.

As I was writing this chapter, I was flying from San Francisco to Minneapolis for a special two-day event that I had the opportunity to keynote (both days!). Upon landing, the person to my left was passing her unfinished glass of water to the flight attendant over me, with my laptop open. . . . I think you know where this is going. During the would-be baton pass, someone missed, and the result was water all over my keyboard.

As a geek, I did all the instant things one can do. Long

story short, the keyboard failed later that evening. Since I was traveling, and this chapter was due, I made the call to get a new laptop. When I showed up at the local Apple store, I was asked why I was buying it and why I didn't need the usual setup help. I explained the circumstances as best I could to a stranger who I'm not sure really wanted to know the answer to her question. But then the strangest thing happened.

She listened—with intent and curiosity. At some point, she asked if I practiced "gratitude." She followed up with, "I could tell you are thankful. I just wondered if you practice it as part of your life." The answer was at that moment, the only truth I could give her: "It's funny and also wonderful you say that. Yes! I'm learning how to practice it. It's changing my life for the better!" The truth is that I was actually writing this chapter and was delayed with the need for a new system. The point of this—I had just finished writing a personal list of everything I was grateful for. And, for some awesome and inexplicable reason, the person who helped me picked up on it. So, write this list. Now and then do it with regularity, perhaps schedule once per month.

Start every day with reciting some positive affirmations. Inspirational quotes are great for this. I've started the chapters of this book with some of my favorites. Spend some time to gather a set of your own. You'll find the process uplifting and then reap the rewards every day from now on.

 **Use your mindfulness.** We can apply our new mindfulness to catching ourselves in the act of being negative, taking conscious charge of how we interpret situations. We'll get better at this over time by asking ourselves, when we're starting to feel negativity:

Am I really in the moment?

Am I finding the good in the moment?

What positives can I choose to focus on?

M.J. Ryan, author of *Attitudes of Gratitude,* makes an interesting observation about how this boosts our spirits. "Where we notice what's right instead of what's wrong, it makes us feel . . . that we have everything we need at least in this moment." He advises to always ask ourselves, "What's right with this wrong?"[15]

The Power of Positive Doing

The power of positive thinking comes first from how it trains our minds to be more open and alert to opportunities, and then from how it guides our actions. I want to be clear that I'm not advocating that it's a mystical matter of the universe rewarding us for our positive thoughts. As I said, I'm no expert on how the universe works, so it's not my place to debunk that notion. What I do think is important is not leaving one's destiny up to such fortuitous intervention. If it comes, wonderful! But we shouldn't let hoping for it mean we are waiting for it. Remember, Wallace Wattles wrote that "[a] man's way of doing things" follows from the way one thinks; the true power of positivity is in what it spurs us to do.

Energize

©freestocks.org

Much has been written about the *Law of Attraction*, a centuries-old precept that suggests "like attracts like." The Law is said to have originally been taught by the Buddha.[16] He wanted his followers to understand that "what you have become is what you have thought." The emphasis in the Buddhist teaching is on how we have the power within our own mind, within ourselves, to translate our thoughts, *and actions*, into reality.

I'm sure we've all experienced how our thinking can seem to conjure up its own reality, for good and for bad. For example, if you're attempting to paddleboard for the first time, and you think you're going to fall, you will. Happened to me! And I even cracked a rib as a result!

On the flip side, I'm sure you've experienced wanting something so badly that you've thought and thought about it, and maybe even visualized it showing up, and then it did! Maybe that was the result of your positive thoughts, or maybe of sheer luck. About that, we can't really know.

But what we can know is that expecting something to happen just because we want it to, and will it to, is a high-stakes game of chance. The much better odds come from visualizing and thinking positively about what you want to happen and *then* putting in the work to manifest your vision.

I want to strike a careful balance here. It's heartening to think that everything you want or need can be satisfied by believing in an outcome, repeatedly thinking about it, and maintaining positive emotional states to *attract* the desired outcome. And there may be something to that. But what I think is more compelling about the Law of Attraction is what it says about our own power within to bring either the positive or the negative into our lives and the world around us.

Have you ever been out somewhere, and someone, for some strange reason, catches your eye? You look and suddenly make eye contact and then quickly look away. You look around, away, down—but there's something pulling you, you can't help but to look again; you have to see if that eye contact will happen again. And then it does?! Whenever that's happened to me, I've thought that perhaps that person and I are meant to know one another, and maybe even to accomplish something together. I'm not without all sense of forces beyond our knowing being at play in the universe.

Energize

©Christin Hume

But when it comes to the Law of Attraction, I'm more interested in how we generate effects on others, which then rebound to us. Whether we are happy or angry, frustrated, or anxious, we emanate our feelings outward to those we're with, even if we're trying to hide them. Human beings are exquisitely finely tuned when it comes to perceiving emotion. That's why if you're feeling particularly happy, even if you're not smiling or showing it obviously in some way, someone might tell you that you're glowing. If you're upset, those around you will pick up on that, which is why people often ask us what's the matter even when we think we're putting on a great poker face. The emotional tone of our thoughts radiates from us whether we know it or not. Others pick up on it and that shapes our interactions and can have a big impact on what happens in our lives.

> ~~Whether we are happy or angry, frustrated, or anxious, we emanate our feelings outward to those we're with, even if we're trying to hide them.~~

We can either allow our thoughts and feelings to be impulsive reactions or we can be intentional about what we're broadcasting.

As for luck, I'm a big fan. But I subscribe to the old saying, "He who is lucky realizes that 'luck' is the point where preparation meets opportunity," often credited to Roman philosopher Seneca the Younger (4 BC–65 AD).[17] Some fascinating recent research has backed this up.

Psychologist Richard Wiseman conducted a 10-year study into the nature of luck entitled, "The Luck Factor."[18] Wiseman found that, to a large extent, people make their own good and bad fortune. In his work, he found that it is possible to enhance the amount of luck that people encounter in their lives.

> To a large extent, people make their own good and bad fortune.

Lucky people generate their own good fortune via four basic principles. They are skilled at creating and noticing chance opportunities, make lucky decisions by listening to their intuition, create self-fulfilling prophesies via positive expectations, and adopt a resilient attitude that transforms bad luck into good.

©Amy Reed

That process of transformation is best done through focused effort. I love a saying about this attributed to Thomas Jefferson: "I am a great believer in luck, and I find the harder I work, the more I have of it."

If you wait for the universe to deliver what you're seeking, you are not taking control of your destiny. I, too, want to believe that my positivity will shower me with rewards. I just don't believe that working to shape one's destiny cancels out opportunities for such benevolence or for serendipity.

You are the architect of your life. You have to design it, plan it, and build it into what you want it to be. Our powers to do so, when we think positively, are truly astonishing.

A New Way to Sing

Allow me to share a wonderful and inspiring story about the power of positivity and how profoundly we can reshape our neural pathways.

> You are the architect of your life. You have to design it, plan it, and build it into what you want it to be. Our powers to do so, when we think positively, are truly astonishing.

It's the story of Mandy Harvey.[19] I was first introduced to this lovely young woman when she performed during the 2017 season of *America's Got Talent*.[20] Harvey was one of five artists that season to earn what's called "The Golden Buzzer." Each of the judges only gets one "Golden Buzzer" per season and it advances the contestant forward regardless of how the other judges vote.

Just before Mandy's performance, the much-maligned and sometimes cynical judge (and producer) Simon Cowell asked her to share her story. What it took for her to stand on that stage is something I'll never forget.

"What's your name?" Simon asked.

"I'm Mandy Harvey," she cheerfully responded while motioning her hands just in front of the ukulele she's wearing.

"And, who's this?" He asked while pointing to his left.

"My interpreter," she responded.

"Okay Mandy, I think I worked this out. So, you're deaf?" he questioned.

"Yes. I lost all my hearing when I was 18 years old," she explained.

The whole audience sighed.

"Wow." He paused. "And, how old are you now?"

"29. So, it's 10 years."

The camera panned to the stage wings where her proud, nervous father was looking on.

"Wow." Cowell paused again. "Mandy, how did you lose your hearing, if you don't mind me asking?"

"I have a connective tissue disorder, so basically, I got sick and my nerves deteriorated," she shared.

Simon then asked, "So, you were singing before you lost your hearing?"

"I've been singing since I was 4. So I left music after I lost my hearing. Then I figured out how to get back into singing with muscle memory, using visual tuners and trusting my pitch."

Judge Howie Mandel then jumped up and exclaimed, "So your shoes are off because you're feeling the vibration, is that how you're following the music?"

"Yeah, I'm feeling the tempo, the beat, through the floor," she confirmed. She had taught her brain to find a new way to listen to music.

Simon put his hands together as if he was to pray and asked, "Mandy, what are you going to sing?"

"I'm going to sing a song that I wrote called, 'Try.'"

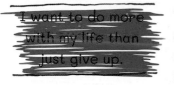
~~I want to do more with my life than just give up.~~

"Okay. Can you tell us what it's about?" Simon inquired, now resting his chin on his folded hands.

"After I lost my hearing, I gave up. But I want to do more with my life than just give up."

At this point the audience roared. Everyone wanted her to do well. But I think part of the thrill was that we all give up sometimes and we all know we should keep going.

Simon sat back, smiled, and said, "Good for you. Good for you. Look, this is your moment and good luck."

Mandy then turned to the side of the stage and waved for her accompanying musicians, a keyboardist and bass player, to join her. Her father looked on with great concern.

The music started, and then Mandy's angelic voice shocked the audience. It was an unforgettable *wow* moment. As the camera panned across the audience, many audience members wiped tears from their eyes. When Mandy belted out, "So, I will try!", the audience and judges leapt to their feet. Her voice trembled as she became overcome with the love . . .

Honestly, I never think I'm going to be surprised or amazed by people. And then you turn up. Just the fact that you are you.

Energize

The room erupted in a long, standing ovation as Mandy smiled with tears of joy and relief.

After the applause finally died down, Simon sat down and with the biggest grin, said to her, "Mandy, I don't think you're going to need a translator for this." He then reached over the judge's panel and hit the golden buzzer. The crowd erupted with another standing ovation.

Mandy placed her hands on the side of her face and broke down into a state of elation and disbelief. Her father cupped his hands and placed them over his mouth as he watched.

Golden confetti filled the air and showered Mandy and the stage.

Simon hugged the interpreter.

Mandy's proud father rushed to hug and congratulate her.

Cowell then approached the stage, held her, gave her two thumbs up, looked her in her eyes and told her, "You know, I've done this a long time. That was one of the most amazing things I've ever seen and heard."

When he sat back down, he left Mandy with these words of appreciation and encouragement: "Honestly, I never think I'm going to be surprised or amazed by people. And then you turn up. Just the fact that you are you. But I think it was your voice, your tone, the song was beautiful . . . congratulations, you are straight through to the live show. Mandy, we found each other."

I wanted to share this story not only because it's a deeply moving example of how we can retrain our brains. It's also a story of the sheer determination to stay positive in order to pursue one's purpose.

In 2013, Mandy earned the opportunity to sing at the Kennedy Center[21] as part of a special concert in celebration of the 23rd anniversary of the Americans with Disabilities Act and National Council on Independent Living Conference.[22] There's a moment where she shares a more intimate look at her darker days, when she lost her hearing and how, and when she finally was able to picture her future as a singer and her purpose in returning to it.

> When I was losing my hearing when I was in music school, I got really depressed as you could probably imagine. And, I just stopped doing music. I didn't feel the need anymore. I didn't want to anymore. It just didn't feel right. But, every day, I sat in my room by myself. I sang this song over and over and over again. The meaning behind it, I guess it's supposed to be happy, but it's not for me. It's more like, I'm not in that good place yet. I'm not there, but I can see it in the future and I know that I need to smile through this. I need to make it okay. I just want to encourage you . . . there are so many challenges in life that you feel like you can't get over and this is your moment. You can't just let it go because it's difficult. If you have a dream, you do it. If it's different or if it changes, then go around, find a different road, but find the finish line. And, smile through it. It's going to be okay.

She then went on to sing a song called *Smile*, an instrumental piece originally written by Charlie Chaplin in 1936 for the film *Modern Times*. Later, John Turner and Geoffrey Parsons added lyrics to it, giving the song a sense of melancholy and then optimism. *Smile* served as the title track to her debut album and her life. The song reminds us that even

> If you have a dream, you do it. If it's different or if it changes, then go around, find a different road, but find the finish line.

in the most challenging, darkest or scariest of times, we are faced with an important choice. We either fret, grieve, shut down, or we smile and work our way toward a more productive, promising and rewarding path. I mean, what's the using of crying when a smile can change everything?

> **"My passion, the whole reason why I sing, is so that I can say, 'Hey, this is what I've done; I really hope that I can encourage you to do the same.'"**

Mandy once told the BBC[23] in its feature on her, "I sing to encourage other people; that's what makes me happy. My passion, the whole reason why I sing, is so that I can say, 'Hey, this is what I've done; I really hope that I can encourage you to do the same.'"

You did Mandy and you do.

Mandy said that what kept her trying was that she could see being able to sing again in her future. Her story is a stirring testament not only to the power of positivity, but to the power of visualization, the practice of conjuring up a detailed, vivid image of the outcome we want to achieve. As a visual thinker, it's a process I threw myself into as I worked on reigniting my creativity, and it was so inspiring and energizing that I will introduce it to you as the next step in lifescaling. Even those of you who think you're just not the visualization type will find it intensely motivating. Let me show you.

VISUALIZE

> "Learn to see, and then you'll know that there is no end to the new worlds of our vision."
> –The Teachings of Don Juan *by Carlos Castaneda*

Visioning is the process of generating images of desired outcomes. The idea is to make the images so vivid that they act as intensely compelling motivators, inspiring belief in our ability to perform to the high level we've envisioned.[1] The practice of mental visioning is common in sports training, with athletes encouraged to create a movie in their heads of performing well. You visualize what success looks and feels like, as if you're an actor stepping into the role of the life you desire. Once you see vividly in your mind's eye the goal you're aiming for, and the process of achieving it, you can't unsee it. Visioning is turning positive thinking into a story of success.

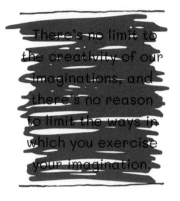

There are many established methods of visioning. I'm going to focus here on the ones I found most engaging and helpful. I hope you will try them, but you should also explore other sources if you're intrigued. As Carlos Castaneda says, there's no limit to the creativity of our imaginations, and there's no reason to limit the ways in which you exercise your imagination.

I do want to make one cautionary observation about the way visioning is sometimes characterized. The power comes not from envisioning just a positive outcome and, having done so, expecting that it will manifest itself. The power comes from also envisioning the *process* of achieving the outcome and motivating us to keep working toward the goal. A good visioning practice includes creating an action plan. The detailed vision of what you want to achieve and how you will do so leads to invaluable realizations about what the journey will require. It helps you anticipate challenges you'll encounter and prepare for them. It also allows you to play out various scenarios and select from them the path you're going to follow.

©Tarik Haiga

I first learned about the remarkable power of envisioning how a journey will unfold through working on my book *X: The Experience Meets Design*. I hired former Pixar artist Nick Sung to help me learn the Disney/Pixar storyboarding process. I wanted to investigate how storyboarding could be used to help companies understand their customers' needs, desires, and life experiences better and serve them more thoughtfully. Ultimately, I used the Disney/Pixar methods to create a visual story of an ideal day in the life of customers. Companies I've taught the process to have found it incredibly helpful in discovering ways to innovate and offer new products and services and more delightful experiences.

I found the process so inspiring that I decided to reboot the entire *X* project, drawing on the lessons I'd learned in visual communication to make the book a novel kind of reading experience that emulated a mobile device on paper, much more visually alive and immersive than my prior books.

The process taught me so much about how visualizing a story allows you to anticipate all sorts of twists and turns events might take, and discover ways you can shape a story to make it more captivating. It also gives you a preview of what those experiencing the story will be going through, highs and lows, and how they can best prepare for inevitable setbacks, as well as helping to believe in the desired outcome.

I can't help but mention that storyboarding contributed greatly to the success of my hero Walt Disney. He invented the practice in the 1920s, when he developed the Mickey Mouse shorts *Plane Crazy* and *Steamboat Willie.* He turned it into a true art form for crafting *Snow White*,[2] and the practice quickly became essential in the planning of all forms of movies.

I mention storyboarding because it exemplifies putting visualization *in action*; it is about all the steps of the journey—for an animated film, literally moment to moment—and learning how believable and thrilling that story can be.

In one way, shape, or form, I now engage in a process of visualization for almost every project I take on. I begin with a vision of the desired outcome and then develop a roadmap that outlines how to get there. If you're interested in doing that and think you'd like to give it a try, I encourage you wholeheartedly. Don't worry if you think you don't have the artistic talent needed for it. As Eric Goldberg,[3] Supervising Animator for the Genie character in Disney's *Aladdin*, says, "A great storyboard artist isn't necessarily Michelangelo."

Even very rough sketches are just fine for the purposes of lifescaling. To see how effective even the simplest stick figure drawings can be for working out ideas, you could check out Dan Roams' book *The Back of the Napkin* and online tutorials on his website Napkin Academy. To learn the storyboarding process, you can find a wealth of tutorials online.

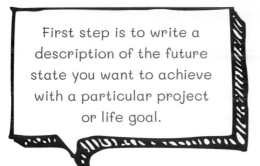

First step is to write a
description of the future
state you want to achieve
with a particular project
or life goal.

I want to introduce here instead the process for visualization that has become my go-to method. The first step is to write a description of the future state you want to achieve with a particular project or life goal. To do that, assemble your work from the values and purpose exercises for inspiration. Now, choose a goal to envision. One I did this for was to come up with the concept for my next book, which had become such a struggle. The articulation of the concept and a visualization for it are now sitting on the easel next to my desk.

© Pimpak

Now, write a vivid description of the outcome you want to achieve. This can be as short or long as necessary to articulate your vision with enough detail. A good gauge of it being detailed enough is that someone who knew nothing about your aims for this endeavor would be able to envision the outcome themselves by reading it. To clarify, I'll share the example that drew me into this practice. I learned about it in a funny way—because of my love of bacon. Yes, bacon.

For my birthday, a friend who knew me very well signed me up for a year of Bacon Club, a gift that just kept on giving throughout the year. Each month, I'd receive a different selection of gourmet bacon and each month, I grew more curious about the company sending it. The packaging was clever, and the bacon "All-Stars" refrigerator magnet and the *Pocket Book of Bacon* that came with the membership were brilliantly illustrated, creative, and actually informative.

I decided to learn about the company, Zingerman's.[4] It's a family of small food-related companies and entrepreneurial ventures located in Ann Arbor, Michigan. After clicking around the site, and ordering more goodies from several of their companies, I learned that one of the ventures, ZingTrain, is a consultancy that helps teach entrepreneurs and executives "Zingerman's model."[5] I further learned that the company employs almost 700 and generates over $55 million annually.

ZingTrain offers public and private seminars on a range of business-related topics, ranging from customer service and leadership to marketing and HR. After reading more, I stumbled across this line:

How unexpected. I needed to know more, and digging a little further into the site, I found a wonderful description of the Zingerman visioning process, offered by Ari Weinzweig, co-founding partner of the company. He describes

> A vision is a picture of the success of a project at a particular time in the future.

Visualize

how visioning has been a core driver of the company's success and describes the features of a good vision description this way:[6]

A vision is a picture of the success of a project at a particular time in the future. A vision is not a mission statement. We see those as being akin to the North Star, a never-ending piece of work that we commit to going after for life. It also isn't a strategic plan—which is the map to where we want to go. A vision is the actual destination. It's a vivid description of what "success" looks and feels like for us—what we are able to achieve, and the effect it has on our staff. We start our planning work with a draft of a positive vision of the future.

An effective vision needs to be:

Inspiring. To all that will be involved in implementing it.

Strategically sound. That is, we actually have a decent shot at making it happen.

Documented. You really need to write your vision down to make it work.

Communicated. Not only do you have to document your vision, but if you want it to be effective you actually have to tell people about it, too.

Weinzweig also shares an actual example the company used to launch a new initiative in 2005 that's been very successful.

A Thursday evening Farmer's Market in the parking lot of Zingerman's Roadhouse—The Vision:

Throngs of people are milling around the Roadhouse parking lot on this Thursday, amazed and excited at the abundance of locally produced goods and services ranging from several varieties of tomatoes to handmade soap and artisan crafts, to herbs and plants, plus Zingerman's items—cheese from the Creamery, breads from the Bakehouse and the ever-energetic Roadshow crew caffeinating all the vendors and customers. Every vendor is selling the best of what they are growing or producing.

There's a tangible truth patrons have come to trust—that all these products have a story and none of them traveled far to get here. Tents and awnings cover the stalls, creating a colorful and festive mood. There are 15–20 vendors at the West Side Farmer's Market so it's accessible and maintains variety but remains magnetic and welcoming.

The Market continues to provide customers with the best products available and serves as a catalyst for community development by offering an educational component and a local music scene. We have space reserved for weekly acts, including local musicians, demonstrations and other activities. Several people recognize the Roadhouse chefs selecting vegetables from the Market's vendors for their weekend's menus. The Market is a family event, where parents bring their children to shop for fresh produce and enjoy a snack at our picnic tables. Guests are thrilled with the produce, the chance to visit with neighbors, and best of all, connect with the farmers who actually grow their food.

This year, the planning committee is generating support throughout the business community. Local businesses hang posters about the Market and participate in promotions. These companies recognize the potential for the Market to draw additional patrons to the area, enabling the Market to become a more self-sustaining entity.

The Market planning committee operates under an inspiring mission statement and is taking steps toward making it a fiscally independent operation. The Market manager is working closely with the Zingerman's liaison to ensure organization and success, from honing job descriptions to developing and proposing paid Market positions. We have a great group of vendors working together who are already excited to build on these successes for next year. Visions and action steps are laid out for the coming years at our annual Market debrief.

Weinzweig attests, "It's pretty much exactly what happened when we started the season for the Market," and he says this process has helped the company create success after success that he believes would not have been possible without the inspiration and the clarity of the vision.

> Make it realistic, but also fantastical. Make it ambitious, but attainable. Make it romantic, but also practical. And whatever you do, make it heartfelt.

The key takeaways are: Make it realistic, but also fantastical. Make it ambitious, but attainable. Make it romantic, but also practical. And whatever you do, make it heartfelt.

Go ahead and write your vision now. Then come back here and we'll take the next step.

Bring Your Vision to Life in Images

Okay, now that you have your vision articulated, it's time to visualize it by actually picturing it, and creating a vision board. This is a visual representation of your life goals that includes images and perhaps also words or phrases to inspire you. There's no one way to do this. Some people clip pictures from magazines and add inspiring words in their handwriting or with cutouts or printed out from their computers. Others, like me, create a digital board using pictures from around the web. Make yours any way you want; after all, this process is about inspiring creativity!

Perhaps this strikes you as a silly exercise—it's viewed that way by plenty of people, and you can find plenty of criticism of the process online. If creating the board were the endpoint of this process, I would be critical too. Vision boards shouldn't be considered a sort of magical totem that will conjure up whatever is pictured on them. But they do have power if they are used to motivate you to take the steps you need to realize your vision.

I was skeptical when I first heard about vision boarding, even though I have used a form of them in my work with companies, to help them craft new experiences for their customers or employees and rally people around the mission. For instance, following the exercises of establishing values and defining purpose, teams would then collaborate to visualize desired outcomes. The process of visualization can help people see and agree on what success looks like. Doing so, brings people together to create a common roadmap that connects their work and goals to results.

I had never used the practice in my own life however. But then my wife and I went through a traumatic experience that left me feeling desperate about ever achieving a goal that was one of the most important to me ever in my life. I'd like to briefly share the story, because the process of creating a vision and action board was so powerful for me and my wife, and I think I would be remiss if I didn't share it.

My wife and I had spent several years trying to adopt a baby. At the beginning, we stayed hopeful, even though we lost out on a number of promising opportunities. We felt sure we'd eventually be successful. But after three devastating opportunities in a row that seemed like definite prospects fell through, we were losing our faith, resolve and more. Something had to change. We then created a vision board depicting the life we would lead with our new baby and defining the actions we would take differently to get there. Let me be clear; we did not embark on this expecting the universe to "give" us a baby because we were envisioning that gift; we were not at all leaving it to the universe to deliver. We saw the process of vision boarding as a means of healing and restoring our will and belief.

We covered our board with pictures that depicted the road to a happy family, and surrounded the pictures with words of encouragement at important stages. Not only was the process therapeutic, as hoped, it gave us renewed resolve and we persevered.

I'm beyond delighted to say the envisioned day finally arrived for us. We welcomed a newborn baby girl into our lives. Her name is Monroe and she has graced us with even more joy than we ever could have hoped for.

She is the reason I believe in the power of vision boards.

Using images of desired outcomes to inspire us to pursue goals is nothing new, or *new age*. The practice goes back deep into the ancient human past,[7] when our ancestors painted the striking images of wild animals that are still so vibrant on the cave walls of Lascaux and Chauvet in France and the Cave of Altamira in Spain, and many others. Experts believe some cave paintings were visualizations of hunts, perhaps part of a practice of "hunting magic"[8] that was intended to increase the abundance of prey. Maybe those cave dwellers believed in magic; we can't really know. But vision boarding doesn't at all rely on a belief that it evokes some sort of supernatural force to bring about what we desire. I will say that it does have a sort of magic, however, a magic of igniting hope and belief; a magic of motivation.

Now let me share with you the vision board I created to inspire me about writing this book. I constructed it around my pillars of purpose. Those pillars, as a reminder, are . . .

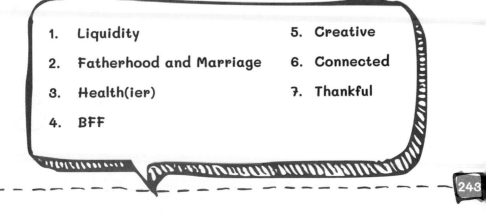

1. Liquidity
2. Fatherhood and Marriage
3. Health(ier)
4. BFF

5. Creative
6. Connected
7. Thankful

Allow me to explain what's on this canvas and why.

From left to right, row by row, hopefully this makes sense and resonates with you.

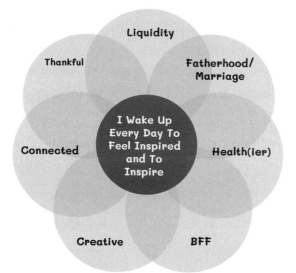

This is a visualization of my pillars of purpose. They serve to remind and inspire me why I'm here and what lifescale is built upon.

This is my (envisioned) family as I see it, standing on a beach, happy, loving and loved, and symbolic of the intentional time we will spend together without distractions or being consumed by overcommitting to work or extracurricular products.

I've not been the healthiest of people, especially as I tried to focus and stay afloat professionally against so many distractions that I allowed in. I see myself fit, eating better, with stronger endurance.

I see myself channeling flow and creating with greater purpose and potency.

I picture my guitars gaining my attention again and I can see that one day, I will finally record my music and offer it to the world.

I have two big goals tied to the release of this book, beyond sharing this moment with you, to help make lifescale a shared movement. I plan on launching a newsletter, a podcast, and a video series aimed at sharing your story and the stories of others, their challenges, and how they're lifescaling. I see the subscriptions and the views growing. The plaque on the right is the memento YouTube sends creators once they hit 100,000 subscribers. I will be there within one-to-two years.

Mother Earth needs us now more than ever. I am making a personal commitment to live greener every day and to join efforts in raising awareness. This will take shape by joining the board of a startup aiming to make bold moves to have strong impact.

Up-level networking

Today, I work behind a screen, on planes, and on stages. I rarely network. My growth and reach stalled as a result. I'm making the conscious investment to get out and join organizations that force me out of my comfort zone. I aim to make meaningful connections and add value to the right community.

A thankful heart is a happy heart

Sometimes with all of the pressure, distraction, and a never-ending list of things to accomplish, I forget to be grateful, to exude appreciation. Sometimes, I've also been short-tempered or self-destructive as a result. Not anymore. I will stay kind, humble, and thankful.

This is an early draft of the book cover. I stared at this every day. This is finally a reality.

The New York Times
BESTSELLER

I picture a future book hitting the official best-seller lists.

Through my work, I aim to inspire personally and professionally and add meaning and significance to everything I create and do. I will also expand my speaking goals to reach conferences, events, and audiences outside of my usual scope to introduce lifescaling to those who can benefit from it. I picture my speaking and lifescale events catapulting my work onto more powerful stages and eventually becoming my sole career.

I picture an engaged community of people learning and sharing lifescale stories and helping one another, where this book and those communities become a catalyst for real world events and workshops.

I see myself speaking at TED and other influential forums like it about lifescaling and the power of creativity against distraction.

I envision a stronger, more consistent connection with important friends who add value to my life and I to theirs. I see my life without friendships that sap my energy or distract me from my lifescale.

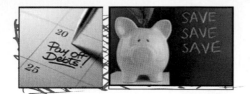

I grew up with debt. I watched my parents take on debt. It was normal to spend money I didn't have on things I didn't need. It was just a way of life. Stuff will no longer weigh me down. I foresee paying off debts and saving money for the things in life that contribute to more quality time and living with family, friends, and professional investments.

I've spent my entire life never believing I was good enough to achieve or earn great things. I'm blessed and fortunate for what I do have today. I've compromised however too greatly in my life and it has cost me opportunities for growth and limited the availability of meaningful choices. I see new opportunities and more powerful choices presenting themselves to me as a result of the actions I take and my intentional dedication to not compromise any longer.

On top of it all, I see love, affection, intimacy and friendship. I lived too long not knowing or appreciating the importance of closeness. I was selfish. I needed this book for a lot of reasons. I see myself growing closer to and fonder of a significant other, an important person, who will never question my intentions, devotion or passion. I also feel that love, fire and companionship in return, without question or doubt.

This is not meant to be a
template for you to follow.
It's just the style that worked
for me. Have fun with this.
Let your creative juices flow.
Embark on an image and
quotation discovery quest.
It's a wonderfully cathartic
and stimulating process. You
feel inspired just seeing and
reading things that connect with you and your goals.
They can come from anywhere that inspires you, but
the three most common sources I found in researching
the experiences of others were favorite magazines and
websites as well as searching keywords on Pinterest and
images on Google.

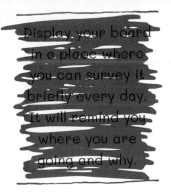

Display your board
in a place where
you can survey it
briefly every day.
It will remind you
where you are
going and why.

Visualize

Display your board in a place where you can survey it
briefly every day. It will remind you where you are going
and why. You're going to experience highs and lows as
you pursue the goals you've portrayed and your board
will keep you focused, driven, and inspired. Every time
you stare at it, you are performing micro-visualization
exercises that directly or indirectly influence your
behavior and activities toward its manifestation.

Do Not Stop There.

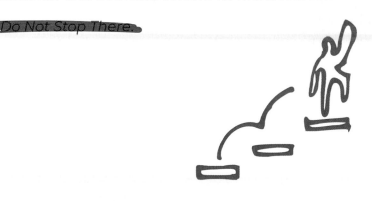

Lights. Camera. Action. Visualizing Your Vision Onto the Lifescale Screen

Now it's time to craft your action plan. Trust me, this is vital, and you will be so pleased when you begin checking off the steps you've listed. There is no better motivation than making progress.

Did you know that research shows people who write out their goals and action steps are 80 percent[9] more likely to achieve them? Experts agree that this is a critical step in the manifestation of your goals. In a fascinating study,[10] as reported by professor of psychology and life coach Neil Farber, college graduates who visualized having their dream job were found to be less likely to get that job than those who visualized a plan for how and where they are going to apply. Farber also writes about another study that found that golfers and tennis players who visualized themselves training were more successful than those who focused their visualization on winning.

Action planning is the process of determining the specific steps you need to take to achieve each goal.[11] I've included a sample action plan template below. In creating such a plan, you can also visualize your action steps. Neil Farber came up with the term *action board* for this.

For each goal you've visualized on your board, prepare an action list of incremental steps that are attainable and measurable. These steps should be clearly defined, as opposed to vague ideas.[12]

Start by writing down the major milestones on your way. You will shortly list a set of the smaller steps that will get you from one to the next of these.

Consider roadblocks or challenges you will face and how to overcome them. Here, think with an open mind about how you can turn problems into challenges and challenges into opportunities.

Review necessary skills, capabilities, resources, or external support you may need.

Define ideal, but realistic, timing for each outcome (target start and realization dates).

Prioritize them and create a timeline.

Create a to-do list of smaller steps for each action to make strides toward your goals.

Get Input

As the Beatles sang, we all need a little help from our friends. Everyone embarking on lifescaling needs friends who will support and positively challenge them. Now that you've articulated your goals and crafted your plan, you can share them easily with others, seeking advice from a

> Everyone embarking on lifescaling needs friends who will support and positively challenge them.

core group of people you trust. Think of them as a board of directors for your lifescaling journey.

©Duy Pham

> Surround yourself with people who push you to do better.

You've got to choose these people carefully. You don't want any cynicism; that's not the kind of challenge you're looking for. You want to limit this to people you know want to see you succeed and who are themselves positive thinkers. Ideally, you've offered them a thoughtful ear and support when they've needed it. Investor Warren Buffet, one of the most successful people of our time, advises, "Surround yourself with people who push you to do better. No drama or negativity. Just higher goals and higher motivation. Good times and positive energy. No jealousy or hate. Simply bringing out the absolute best in each other."[13]

The insight and inspiration people will share can be wonderfully energizing. I had a striking experience of this as I was working on the book.

It was the first day of the fall season and I was lucky enough to have arrived in Lisbon, Portugal, to experience it. The skies were blue, the weather was more summer than fall, but perfect, and a dear friend of mine was also visiting the city. We were both part of a closely knit group of friends who had once seen quite a bit of one another. The last time all of us had gotten together, though, was several years before in London, and we knew then that it would be years, if ever, before we could all be in the same place together again. So far, that's proved true. While I've seen everyone individually at one time and in one country or another, we haven't managed to meet all at once. As for this friend, it had been four years since I'd seen her.

In that time, she had temporarily placed her startup on hold and traveled the world to explore its beauty while also exploring the beauty within herself. She'd also written two books along the way. But what served as the centerpiece for our conversation this particular evening, other than the enchanting scenery that is Lisbon, were the awe-inspiring stories she shared about how in her travels, she set out to embrace spirituality, mindfulness, meditation, and learn and practice the art of creative flow.

One year earlier, I wouldn't have had anything to contribute to the conversation. But by this time, I was well into my lifescaling journey. I was a little hesitant to share my story of having become so overwhelmed by distraction and disconnected from my creativity. She'd been public with her journey, sharing videos, pictures, and posts about what she'd learned, her struggles, her adventures, and the exotic places her quest for meaning had taken her. I, on the other hand, had yet to tell anyone outside my closest personal circle about lifescaling. But her story of reigniting her own creativity was so in sync with the journey I was on that I went ahead and told her all about my discoveries.

She made sharing easy, conveying that she was as genuinely curious about my journey as I was of hers. The conversation consumed a long evening and I left even more inspired about the road I was on and with a wealth of great insight to carry with me.

Opening up to feedback is a great strengthener of our creative muscles.

Some friends and family members you share with may not be supportive of some of your plan. You might hear some doubts and cautions may be offered. Or some people might seem to be just supporting you without really thinking deeply about what you've shared. Don't be discouraged. Opening up to feedback is a great strengthener of our creative muscles. It's one of the hallmarks of what Carol Dweck calls the growth mindset. I'm sure you will also get lots of great encouragement and tips about resources that can be helpful, offers to connect you with people who can assist you, and suggestions of possibilities you might otherwise never have imagined.

I've shared that one of my lifescaling goals has been to do more networking. I decided to use the writing of this book as one occasion for that, and I reached out to a number of people to get feedback. They offered many wonderful suggestions about research to read and shared their own stories of creative struggle, which was all so helpful in honing the concept and discovering some new thinkers whose work has been profoundly mind-opening.

Select those you share with carefully, but trust that by opening up your vision to them, they will help you see it, and achieve it, in invaluable ways. You are the author of the book of your life, but all authors need good editing!

DIVE

Wading through
the Shallows
to Dive into
Deep
Creativity

"You don't get results by focusing on results. You get results by focusing on the actions that produce results."
– Mike Hawkins

Okay, you've got your action plan worked out. Now it's time to apply your renewed ability to focus, your positive thinking and motivational visualization, and your passionate sense of purpose to creative productivity. That requires carving out time for deep dives into creative work. Instead of always treading water in a desperate effort to keep up with the relentless onslaught of distractions, you allow yourself to plunge into the projects that are the most important, and the most meaningful, to you.

For so many of us, when we do give ourselves time for creative work, we don't take the deep plunge. It's like we're snorkeling rather than scuba diving. We just don't think we can afford to take the time to really go deep. That's in part because we don't realize how productive we can be during creative work sessions if we are truly, utterly focused.

We tend to think that creative output requires a large time commitment. And we're concerned that if we fail to answer all, or at least most, of our emails, take phone calls when we get them, and process through all of the flotsam and jetsam of bureaucratic paperwork (so much of which is online now), we'll find ourselves drowning.

The truth is that most of us do have to keep up with a large volume of basic work tasks and we do have to be responsive to messages and calls. We have to get paperwork done on time and we can't just beg off on all, or even most, meetings.

> To make time for deep creative work, we have to master the art of switching from the shallows to the depths.

So in order to make time for deep creative work, we have to master the art of switching from the shallows to the depths. What's vital is to establish a basic pattern to your days for moving from deep concentration on creative projects, to attention to all of the routine demands you've got to keep up with.

Professor Cal Newport of Georgetown University has written several books on personal and professional performance, and he addressed the need to develop the ability to switch back and forth from the shallows to the depths in his 2016 book *Deep Work*. He has inspiring things to say about the payoffs of deep work, which

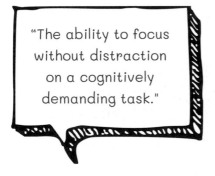

> "The ability to focus without distraction on a cognitively demanding task."

he defines as, "the ability to focus without distraction on a cognitively demanding task. It's a skill that allows you to quickly master complicated information and produce better results in less time."

Newport is a computer scientist and he has studied the advance of the "second machine age" in which robots will be taking over so much work. He highlights that the ability to get into deep work mode is becoming ever-more important not only because of the epidemic of distraction but because the better we are at deep work, the more competitive advantage we will have in performing the jobs that even very smart machines won't be able to perform. He posits what he calls his Deep Work Hypothesis:[1]

> *The ability to perform deep work is becoming increasingly rare at exactly the same time it is becoming increasingly valuable in our economy. As a consequence, the few who cultivate this skill, and then make it the core of their working life, will thrive.*

The heartening news he shares about this is that the ability to dive deep isn't something that's just bestowed by birth on some *crème de la crème* of the super-focused. It's a skill that we can all learn with practice.

©Paula May

Key to this is what Newport refers to as "alt tabbing" between shallow and deep work. How does he distinguish between them?

Deep Work = *Professional activities performed in a state of distraction-free concentration that push your cognitive capabilities to their limit. These efforts create new value, improve your skill, and are hard to replicate.*

Shallow Work = *Noncognitively demanding, logistical-style tasks, often performed while distracted. These efforts tend not to create much new value in the world and are easy to replicate.*

He outlines a number of basic approaches for toggling. They're not mutually exclusive, and I've been experimenting with all of them. You should, too, and you can adjust your approach as best fits your work situation over time.

The Monastic Philosophy: This approach is based on the practice of monks of retreating to isolation, renouncing worldly pursuits to devote all of their time to spiritual work.[2] The idea is to protect yourself from all distraction by physically removing yourself to a quiet place and unplugging, for at least one or more days, to allow yourself the space and time to engage in uninterrupted work.

The Bimodal Philosophy: Here, you're balancing between monastic self-imposed exile and everyday social and professional engagement. You schedule a large block of time entirely away from the shallows of your everyday work every day, which is often best to do in the morning, and then attend to everything else for the remainder for the day.

The Rhythmic Philosophy: Here you're oscillating more frequently between deep and shallow work, so in shorter increments of time. A version of the Pomodoro technique would be a great way to create a rigorous pattern for this, perhaps dedicating several 90 minute blocks a day to deep work and coming up for check-ins with email and all in the time in between.

The Journalistic Philosophy: This is for when carving out substantial chunks of time in advance for deep work is simply not possible. We train ourselves to get into deep work mode quite quickly and take advantage of any opportunities as they come. It's named after a journalist's need to dig deep to focus and crank out a story on deadline in very little time and even with lots of noise going on all around them.

This one takes more practice. I've struggled with it but am beginning to find that I can get back into creative work more and more quickly and take good advantage of unexpected moments without demands on my time, such as when takeoff of a flight is delayed for 15 or 20 minutes. I can pull out my laptop and get right back into writing and get some significant work done that I've found I am happy with later.

Depending on the nature of your work, there are probably always going to be some days or weeks when you can't schedule much if any creative deep time. But this journalistic approach is not optimal, and you should strive not to let this become your default mode for deep work.

Ritualize the Dedication of Time and Space

It's said that greatness is founded on establishing a routine and the discipline to keep to it. As you work to establish your toggling system, be ruthless about time you have scheduled for your deep dives. Give that time up only for truly urgent demands.

Greatness is founded on establishing a routine and the discipline to keep to it.

This is hard. I know. I struggled mightily with it. It's such a fight not only because of intrusions, but because of what I call the cult of busyness. The work world has glorified being busy as a badge of honor, and we've learned to believe we have to *show* people we're really busy. If we're not emailing or on the phone or in a meeting, how can they see that we're busy?

©Lost Co

Busyness is distraction masquerading as productivity. If you make deep time and increase the quality of your output, trust me, no one will care how busy you look. Or, actually, they'll be amazed

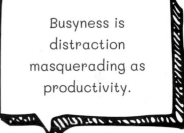

Busyness is distraction masquerading as productivity.

and impressed by what you've been able to produce even though you didn't seem to be crazy busy. There is no prize for answering x emails or attending y meetings every day. There's no reward for self-inflicted burnout.

A few key things made dedicating myself to scheduled deep work time much easier for me.

©Artiom Vallat

Establish a dedicated space. Find a place away from work and home that you can escape to. I tried locking myself in a conference room at my office and taking coffee/water/snack breaks or bathroom runs only when I knew there would be no one around for chitchat. That did help, but I found that the distractions of the office still invaded my mind. All of the sudden I'd find myself thinking about a client meeting or a report I had to get done instead of the project I had decided to focus on. My home office was worse. It's strewn with stacks of paperwork that always need filing, receipts to organize, bills to pay, and when my adorable daughters are home, I always want to go and play with them.

Some people find working at cafes does the trick. That wasn't possible for me. Their hubbub doesn't serve as focus-inducing white noise for me as I know it does for some people. I find myself listening to conversations, even if I put on headphones. Cafes are just filled with so many interesting people to ogle over!

Eventually, I began allocating regularly scheduled time to visit a small place in Lake Tahoe. I got the idea from the extraordinary creative producer J.K. Rowling, author of the *Harry Potter* books.

Guests at the five-star Balmoral Hotel in Edinburgh[3] pay upwards of £1000 to stay in room 552, much more than the rate for other rooms. Why? Because that's where Rowling famously checked herself in to finish the final volume of the *Harry Potter* series. In an interview with Oprah Winfrey[4] in 2010, Rowling explained how she needed to remove herself from everyday life to stimulate deep creativity.

> ... there came a day, the window cleaner came, the kids were at home, the dogs were barking and I could not work. And, this lightbulb went off in my head, and I thought, I can throw money at this problem. I can now solve this problem. For years and years and years, I could go to a cafe and sit in a different kind of noisy work. I thought, I could go to a quiet place.

Going to Tahoe worked for me largely because it was such a significant gesture. It's a four-hour drive from my home in the San Francisco Bay area and it cost quite a chunk of change. But I have friends who have converted garden sheds available at Lowe's and Home Depot for several hundred dollars into creative studios right in their backyards. Other friends have rented campsites and set up a pop-up creative shop complete with batteries, solar recharging stations, and even generators.

Consider making an investment in a getaway space as you begin to develop your deep work rituals. This can be a great shock to the creative system, forcing it to focus and providing fantastic positive reinforcement about how valuable disciplined deep time will be.

I found that once I had built up my deep work muscles this way, I was able to focus deeply at the office, too, and even at home. I'd lock myself in a room in the basement and come out only for pre-timed breaks.

©Stil

Establish the Time and Scope of Sessions. It's also extremely helpful to plan the duration of your sessions and to set a goal for your output per session. I would dedicate sessions to completing specific sections of the chapters of this book, with a rigorous plan for word count, and as I learned how much time it would take me, with my new focus, to write the amount of words that I was happy with, I fine-tuned my scheduling of sessions accordingly.

Construct a Creativity Support System. Gather everything you will need to help you keep your energy up and stay comfortable and focused during your sessions and make sure you've prepared the environment. Obviously, turn off your email and phone. That's your bare minimum environmental control. I always bring my favorite monitor with me; make sure I have coffee, water, and some snack food at hand (and sometimes champagne, if I'm feeling celebratory, like if I'll be finishing a chapter); bring an exercise recording so that I can take quick workout breaks by my desk; classical, old school jazz and lo-fi music playlists loaded; and if I'm working in a public space, headphones.

What would your list look like?

My list:

The Value of not Working Alone

Once you have developed your ability to reliably dedicate yourself to deep work in your dedicated getaway space, you should try spending some creative time in one of the wealth of open workspaces that have cropped up. This allows for working in a manner Cal Newport calls the *hub-and-spoke* model. The idea is to place yourself in a creative space with others who possess disparate skillsets, mindsets, and goals.

Place yourself in a creative space with others who possess disparate skillsets, mindsets, and goals.

Working in these spaces can be challenging at first. They can be like cafes, with lots of conversations, clanking of glasses, and hubbub of chairs being moved around. But whereas at cafes, usually most people are there to enjoy cappuccino and pastries, or have meetings, with only a minority there to work alone, in open workspaces everyone is there primarily to work. You're surrounded by people who also need to toggle between deep and shallow work. That creates the opportunity to make great creative use even of your shallow time. Because open workspaces are talent pools.

The idea of a hub-and-spoke model is to have a dedicated quiet space for doing your deep work, which most of the spaces offer, and then to plug into the serendipity of the space to stoke creativity by exposing yourself to all sorts of interesting people doing interesting things during the time you come up for air. Meeting other people engaged in creative work can be so stimulating. Creativity is buzzing all around you, and you are perked up by the creative energy. You meet people working on some of the most amazing projects, and they can share ideas that can help you take your work in even more exciting directions. Such encounters often lead to creative collaborations. Working in these spaces can also create a healthy sense of competition, encouraging you to get the most out of your deep work dives so that when you emerge you feel pleased with yourself and a rightful member of this creativity hub.

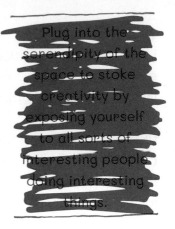

Plug into the serendipity of the space to stoke creativity by exposing yourself to all sorts of interesting people doing interesting things.

©Angelo Pantazis

I learned the benefits of working in a creativity hub early in my writing career. As I was developing the manuscript for *Engage!*, I leased a second office space to place myself right in the thick of the creative outburst that would come to be called Web 2.0. All around me, people were creating the innovations that have so profoundly shaped our lives. The building was located in the San Francisco SoMa district, on Second St., and was packed with tech startups. Creativity coursed through the place. Innovation was happening in every room. The concentration of game-changing companies and leaders, both in my building and across the street in South Park and around the neighborhood in many converted open workspaces was incredible. Simply going out to get lunch or dinner, or to pick up coffee, you couldn't help but overhear people discussing brilliant ideas for some new program or invention that would become the next new big thing.

I was challenged to push my creative boundaries. I learned powerful new skills, like online design. My point of view broadened and I was constantly inspired. I benefited from so many happy accidents.

If you develop the discipline to dive into deep work within these open work environments, you won't be distracted by all of the activity; you'll be rejuvenated and re-energized for a next deep dive.

©Emma Matthews

Ruthlessly Prioritize

To make time for deep work, you've got to implement a process of extremely strict prioritization of what you will work on, stripping out most, if not all, nonessential obligations and time-sucks.

To make time for deep work, you've got to implement a process of extremely strict prioritization of what you will work on, stripping out most, if not all, nonessential obligations and time-sucks. In researching how highly productive creative people do this, I came upon the story of Fidji Simo, vice president of product at Facebook. Her rapid ascension within the ranks of such a highly competitive company is widely admired within the tech circles. In a profile in *First Round Review*,[5] she shares lessons she had learned about creative productivity when she was facing what threatened to be a long stretch of downtime.

She manages a team of 400 product managers and engineers developing some of the most successful products that we all, for better or for worse, use on a regular basis. Just a couple of years ago, however, she was ordered to bedrest for five months during a complicated pregnancy. At the time, she was in the midst of a number of critical projects, and she decided that she would not take a leave of absence. Instead, she would work from home. She recalled in the article that, "It required immense focus. I actually felt so much more productive than when I was in the office." The article explained:

> Working remotely meant she was forced to say "no" to anything that wasn't critical, which created the time and space—physically and mentally—to put 100% of her effort toward the most pressing and important projects. By cutting out anything nonessential she was able to focus on the most strategic priorities, not only for the product team, but for herself. When she returned, she brought this commitment to focused work with her—eager to share it with her team

We can all benefit from adopting her practices.

- She schedules every aspect of her work, including time for handling unforeseen interruptions. All too often, *urgent* meetings, calls, and emails sneak their way on to your calendar, hogging up critical deep work time. Acknowledge this reality by scheduling some time for intrusions. "My calendar is my most powerful tool for enforcing my prioritization," Simo says. She plans for two hours of "buffer time" each week for unscheduled interruptions, and then she allocates it with strict prioritization, postponing any requests for her time that she can schedule for later. Of course, no one wants to hear that their request, need or time is not important to you. Communicating well here is key. Simo suggests the following ways to respond:

  o **What to say when something can wait:** "I'm focused 100 percent on *x* this week, so if this isn't an urgent issue, let's re-evaluate next week."

  o **What to say when you need a little time:** "I'm fully focused on *x* right now, so I can't meet about that this week. But if you send me an email, I will get back to you with an answer by *y*."

  o **What to say when someone else can handle it:** "This week, I need to focus all my time on *x*, but if you need an urgent answer, you can reach out to my team lead, *z*, who is focused on that issue."

©Martin Shreder

- She concentrates her deep work time entirely on the most important project on her agenda.

- She schedules "clarity" check-ins for herself, between 30 to 60 minutes each, to review her prioritization of tasks and assess if she's on course with her goals and prioritizing right for her team. Simo's drill for this is:

    o List the broader team or organization's top priorities.

    o Check that your personal priorities for the week still align with those priorities.

    o Check for any new information or data that requires a shift in priorities.

    o Check priorities against your time allocation, meetings, and commitments that week.

o Make any adjustments to your calendar to better reflect your priorities.

o Note any priority adjustments that impact or need to be communicated to your team.

You can adapt her process in any way that's best for your work.

· For meetings, which we all know can be such unproductive time thieves, she advises: Have a clear agenda for what you want to achieve or what needs to be achieved in every meeting. Also, maintain a checklist of objectives that you want to leave each meeting with.

· Simo has also, vitally, made time for her personal creative expression. She shared that she is a painter, but she hadn't made time for it in years. She missed the happiness she felt when making her art, and by being so rigorous with her work schedule, she was able to create time for it again. She explained,

> I decided to do one art project a week. You would think finding the time to stick to it was the harder part, but it wasn't. What was hard was realizing that being creative was one of my core goals—it was being honest with myself about my priorities first and then enforcing them going forward.[6]

Diving into Flow

Building your ability to focus creatively is like holding your breath. The more you practice it, the more you increase your ability to hold longer and deeper breaths.

By rigorously carving out time for deep work, you will create the condition for experiencing regular episodes of flow, which can become deeper and richer the more you dive in. Recall that the state of flow is characterized by:

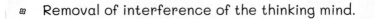

- Removal of interference of the thinking mind.

- Complete involvement in what we are doing.

- A sense of ecstasy—of being outside everyday reality.

- Great inner clarity—knowing what needs to be done, and how well we are doing.

- The confidence that the activity is doable, that one's skills are adequate to the task.

- A total lack of self-consciousness. There's a sense of serenity—no worries about oneself, and a feeling of growing beyond the boundaries of the ego.

- Timelessness—one is so thoroughly focused on the present that hours seem to pass by in minutes.

- Intrinsic motivation—whatever produces flow becomes its own reward.

©Sasha Stories

Mihaly Csikszentmihalyi says[7] *flow* is "a state in which people are so involved in an activity that nothing else seems to matter; the experience is so enjoyable that people will continue to do it even at great cost, for the sheer sake of doing it." That's the ecstasy of it, and the marvelous thing is that we can achieve deeper and deeper experiences of that ecstasy. We can become flow free divers.

Free divers swim to extreme depths underwater (the current record is 214 m) without any breathing apparatus. Champions can hold their breath for extraordinary amounts of time—the record for women is 9 minutes, 11 for men.[8]

Have you ever wondered what pushes the insane progress in adventure sports? I think back to my teens and early 20s growing up in Southern California and surfing Point Dume and Zuma. I think the biggest wave I rode then was a massive wall with a face of four feet. (Hey, that was big for me!) And at the time, I think about the pros who were conquering massive 25-foot waves around the world (especially in Northern California at Mavericks). Nowadays, surfers are pushing more than three times that. In November 2017, Brazilian surfer Rodrigo Koxa broke the Guinness World[9] record by riding an 80-foot wave. This beat the previous record[10] held by American surfer Garrett McNamara (78 feet). These types of incredible leaps forward have been achieved in many sports.

How do these super humans perform these otherwise unimaginable feats? According to Steven Kotler,[11] author of *The Rise of Superman: Decoding the Science of Ultimate Human Performance*, the secret lies in the ability to engage in the state of flow.[12] He highlights that when people are in flow, their "... mental and physical ability go through the roof, and the brain takes in more information per second, processing it more deeply."

Our nervous system is incapable of processing more than about 110 bits of information per second. And in order to hear me and understand what I'm saying, you need to process about 60 bits per second.

That's why when we're in flow, we are totally unaware of distractions. Csikszentmihalyi explains the science of this.[13] "It sounds like a kind of romantic exaggeration," he says. "But actually,

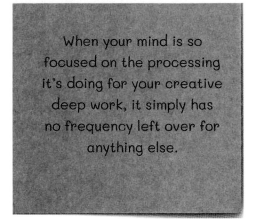

When your mind is so focused on the processing it's doing for your creative deep work, it simply has no frequency left over for anything else.

our nervous system is incapable of processing more than about 110 bits of information per second. And in order to hear me and understand what I'm saying, you need to process about 60 bits per second." He continued, "That's why you can't hear more than two people. You can't understand more than two people talking to you."

When your mind is so focused on the processing it's doing for your creative deep work, it simply has no frequency left over for anything else. Even for noticing while you're in flow that you're in flow.

Whenever I think about this aspect of flow, I can't help but think of a wonderful scene in the movie *Finding Nemo*. Nemo's father, Marlin, is trying to find the East Australian Current, so he can get to Sydney super fast to look for his son. The current is the River Rea, by the way. It's a river within the ocean that's 100 km wide and 1.5 km deep, and though it moves more slowly than is depicted in the film, it courses at an impressive speed of 7 km per hour.

In the scene, Marlin calls out to a turtle racing by near him, "I need to get to the East Australian Current," and the turtle replies, "You're ridin' it dude!"

We can think of the state of flow as what the founder of the field of Positive Psychology, Martin Seligman, calls *optimal experience*, a kind of

> The best moments usually occur when a person's body or mind is stretched to its limits in a voluntary effort to accomplish something difficult and worthwhile.

perfection. He writes, "The best moments usually occur when a person's body or mind is stretched to its limits in a voluntary effort to accomplish something difficult and worthwhile," and that,[14] "Consciousness and emotion are there to correct your trajectory; when what you are doing is seamlessly perfect, you don't need them."[15]

While our creative output will never actually be perfect, we can have a perfect experience while we are making it. And we can even strive to be in flow more often and for longer periods. We can even become what Csikszentmihalyi calls an "autotelic" person,[16] which he describes as being "never bored, seldom anxious, involved with what goes on and in flow most of the time." He further explains,

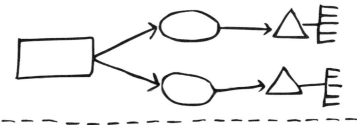

Autotelic[17] is used to describe people who are internally driven, and as such may exhibit a sense of purpose and curiosity. This determination is an exclusive difference from being externally driven, where things such as comfort, money, power, or fame are the motivating force.

We can achieve this state of being by constantly challenging ourselves, strengthening and gaining new skills, opening ourselves up to feedback so that we're aware of how we're performing, and having well-defined success metrics to evaluate our progress.

Keep Score to Keep Improving Your Performance

Cal Newport likens working deeply to the process of business governance. Businesses seek to carefully allocate their investments, of resources and their people's time, in order to maximize their return on those investments (ROI). In order to provide yourself with the feedback you need to evaluate your progress in developing your creative productivity, you've got to devise a way of measuring your return on your time and mental, spiritual resources. I advise creating a creativity scorecard. This tracks daily and weekly measures of achievement of your goals.

> In order to provide yourself with the feedback you need to evaluate your progress in developing your creative productivity, you've got to devise a way of measuring your return on your time and mental, spiritual resources.

This may sound intimidating, but it can be a very simple tracking of where you are versus where you need, or want, to be. Here is an example of the scorecard I used to track my progress in writing this book:

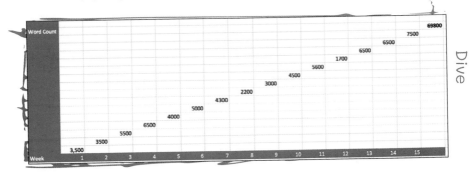

You can't imagine how motivating this simple tracking of word count was to me.

I developed this concept based on the work of Chris McChesney, Sean Covey, and Jim Huling, the authors of the influence book *The 4 Disciplines of Execution*. The book is designed to help business people execute on plans "in the midst of the whirlwind of distractions."[18] Their key tips for scorecards are that they should:

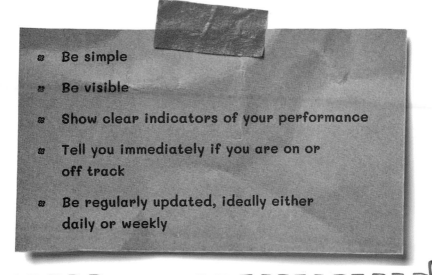

- Be simple

- Be visible

- Show clear indicators of your performance

- Tell you immediately if you are on or off track

- Be regularly updated, ideally either daily or weekly

This simple personal accountability device will allow you to see exactly when you're falling short and that helps pinpoint why. It also lights a fire of creative determination.

To show you how eye-opening this tracking can be, I'll share a very embarrassing earlier version, from when I was struggling to make any progress on the book project I had thought would be my next one. This graphic representation of how far off the mark I was of the goals I had set for myself for the hours needed to generate targeted word counts helped me realize that I had to take a serious look at what was going wrong with my creative process.

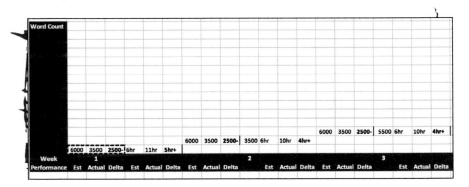

The scorecard shows the words I wrote versus my goal and how much time I spent measured against the time I estimated I would need to write that amount. You can see there are glaring gaps between my goals and actual output. What this scorecard doesn't represent is the number of times I stopped my Pomodoro timer in the middle of a deep work block to chase digital distractions.

The wake-up call I got from this helped me to see 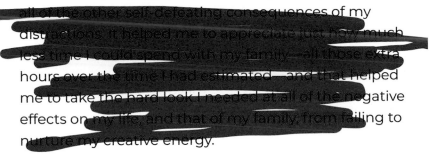 all of the other self-defeating consequences of my distractions. It helped me to appreciate just how much less time I could spend with my family—all those extra hours over the time I had estimated—and that helped me to take the hard look I needed at all of the negative effects on my life, and that of my family, from failing to nurture my creative energy.

On the flip side, once I had begun applying the insights I gained from researching this book, when I set out to go ahead and write it, you can see the steady progress I made. What that scorecard taught me was that there's a great sense of accomplishment in gaining control over your creative productivity, even from the smallest strides toward achieving your goals.

It's important to be diligent about measuring and charting your progress as you go. Measuring your progress not only helps inspire you, it allows you to calibrate the goals you've set for yourself better with your current skills, and that helps you to get into flow.

We get better and better at taking on new challenges, understanding that we've got to apply ourselves to developing skills that will allow us to carefully balance the difficulty of our creative mission with our ability to achieve it.

"It is not enough to be happy, to have an excellent life," Csikszentmihalyi states. "The point is to be happy while doing things that stretch our skills, that help us grow and fulfill our potential." I couldn't describe the goal of lifescaling any better.

"It is not enough to be happy, to have an excellent life. The point is to be happy while doing things that stretch our skills, that help us grow and fulfill our potential."

-Mihaly Csikszentmihalyi

CONCLUSION

The Art of
Lifescaling is
Learning How
to Live, Learn
and Love

"Above all, you keep your clarity. You keep your focus. You keep your sense of love. And, you keep your sense of purpose. . . . A lot of people define success differently. You can have everything. You can have all the money in the world. But, if it's not enjoyable, if it's not sustainable, if you can't be a person of integrity, having all these things, what does it matter? What does it mean? The value is internal. Your value is internal."

- Lauryn Hill

Though we've reached the end of the book, this is not the end of your lifescaling journey, or mine. This is not the finish line. I hope you will now apply this new way of continuous learning and new way of knowing and loving yourself and what truly matters to you to an ongoing lifescaling adventure. I hope these insights and tools will help you continue to evolve, grow and expand your capabilities and horizons.

With each step of this process you're charting a path that will keep sparking your imagination and inspiring brighter futures and meaningful outcomes. You can see and feel so much more now. You're becoming increasingly aware. You're becoming more and more creative. A creative life is a life of endless possibilities and as you flex your imagination and skills, you unlock new achievements, capabilities and esteem.

Creativity becomes the stuff of your life. It's how you think. It's what you see in front of you, what you imagine and in your mind's eye. It's how you express yourself. It's how you make decisions. It's not just about what you create. What also matters is why you create.

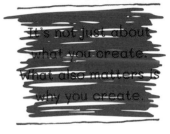

It's not just about what you create. What also matters is why you create.

about what you create. What also matters is why you create. Your purpose, shaped by your values, balanced by self-reflection and consciousness, serve as an evolving center of reference to guide you through the smallest and biggest moments of your life at every lifescale event. More than that, they unlock experiences and opportunities you might not have otherwise had.

©Kelly Sikkema

The Book that Got Written

I couldn't have written this book without the help of lifescaling. Everything I learned, everything it helped me unlearn, everything that helped me focus, open my eyes, reset my center of reference and practice creativity, poured out of me in ways I hadn't experienced in years, if ever, at this magnitude. Truthfully, at the beginning, learning something new, trying to change my life and writing about it, was both debilitating and enlivening. With each chapter however, I found myself progressively visualizing, thinking and expressing at deeper levels. I started writing with such passion that I wrote many more words than I had planned to.

I cut over 50,000 words from the first draft of the manuscript, just about the length of the final book, and I've kept them for a series of companion

I found myself longing for additional ways to create.

projects. My creative productivity was supercharged. My mind, body and spirit were electrified, inspired to the point that when I wasn't writing, I found myself longing for additional ways to create. I didn't want to lose the momentum. I didn't want to stop growing. I had fallen back in love with learning and with expressing myself.

I deeply hope the book will help you enjoy the exhilaration of lifescaling too.

Lifescaling is Your Journey

Lifescaling is a personal exploration into the realms that cloud our being. Lifescaling is also an endeavor toward discovery and vitality. Furthermore, it's an individual covenant, a personal contract to see, learn and practice the things that truly allow you to live your best life. Lifescaling is a way of managing life as life evolves with a commitment and intent to unlock newfound or repressed creativity, foster joy and stoke happiness. It is a voyage of self-discovery, understanding and awakening. And it never needs to end.

The more you know, the more you grow. The more you create, the more you want to create. The more you see, the more you can't unsee. The more you feel, the more you want to feel . . . what you want to feel. The more you love what's inside of you, the more we'll love what you express outside of you. And, the more you know who you are, the more you can become the ideal you.

As you set your mind and soul to what's next, as you create, you gain experience, expertise and perspective. You gain pride, confidence and wisdom. Each iteration of you, sees and feels things the previous version could not.

As such, this really is just the beginning for you, and for me. And, this is exactly what lifescaling is all about. Lifescaling is about growth and development and new awakenings as we journey through our days and nights. It's about finding happiness in our evolution. It's about gaining skills and mental models that help us productively navigate life and work through overwhelming distractions and obstacles. More so, lifescaling helps us create and live creatively.

It's clarity and vision. It's openness and mindfulness. It's intent, focus and the work you do that leads to the little accomplishments every day that add up to big achievements and outcomes throughout your journey.

It's a way of life. It's with you every day. Lifescaling evolves as you evolve. And the truth is that I'm still working on it. And, if you're here, you're working on it too.

Take a moment to breathe, to appreciate the moment, and to remind yourself as you lifescale, "this is what I am working for . . . this moment, right now." For as long as you're learning, growing and creating, wherever you are, is where you're supposed to be.

To continue the journey, please visit www.lifescaling.me.

Notes

Chapter 1

1 https://www.nytimes.com/2013/05/05/opinion/sunday/a-focus-on-distraction.html

2 https://www.ics.uci.edu/~gmark/Home_page/Welcome.html

3 https://childmind.org/article/how-using-social-media-affects-teenagers/

Chapter 2

1 https://www.fastcompany.com/40491939/netflix-ceo-reed-hastings-sleep-is-our-competition

2 https://www.vice.com/en_us/article/vv5jkb/the-secret-ways-social-media-is-built-for-addiction

3 https://www.interaction-design.org/literature/topics/persuasive-design

4 https://www.1843ma gazine.com/features/the-scientists-who-make-apps-addictive

5 https://screentimenetwork.org/apa?eType=EmailBlastContent&eId=5026ccf8-74e2-4f10-bc0e-d83dc030c894

6 https://www.vox.com/2018/8/8/17664580/persuasive-technology-psychology

7 https://www.nytimes.com/roomfordebate/2013/10/09/are-casinos-too-much-of-a-gamble/slot-machines-are-designed-to-addict

8 https://yaleglobal.yale.edu/content/smartphone-addiction-slot-machine-your-pocket

9 http://www.tristanharris.com/essays/

10 https://www.amazon.com/Wired-Child-Reclaiming-Childhood-Digital/dp/150321169X

11 https://www.vox.com/2018/8/8/17664580/persuasive-technology-psychology

12 https://www.independent.co.uk/life-style/gadgets-and-tech/bill-gates-and-steve-jobs-raised-their-kids-techfree-and-it-shouldve-been-a-red-flag-a8017136.html

13 https://techcrunch.com/2017/09/08/meet-the-tech-company-that-wants-to-make-you-even-more-addicted-to-your-phone/

14 https://www.theverge.com/2017/12/11/16761016/former-facebook-

exec-ripping-apart-society

15 https://www.theverge.com/2017/11/9/16627724/sean-parker-facebook-childrens-brains-feedback-loop

16 https://thenextweb.com/apple/2018/01/20/apple-ceo-becomes-latest-tech-bigwig-to-warn-of-social-medias-dangers/

17 https://twitter.com/martyswant/status/960683198463250434

18 https://www.weforum.org/agenda/2016/07/multitasking-is-exhausting-your-brain-say-neuroscientists

19 http://www.businessinsider.com/teen-suicides-outnumber-homicides-smartphones-2017-8

20 http://www.businessinsider.com/teen-suicides-outnumber-homicides-smartphones-2017-8

21 https://www.ted.com/talks/manoush_zomorodi_how_boredom_can_lead_to_your_most_brilliant_ideas

22 https://www.glassdoor.com/employers/blog/science-behind-multitasking-slowly-erodes-productivity/

23 https://hbr.org/2015/06/conquering-digital-distraction

24 https://www.theguardian.com/commentisfree/2018/aug/25/skim-reading-new-normal-maryanne-wolf?CMP=share_btn_fb

25 http://newsroom.ucla.edu/releases/is-technology-producing-a-decline-79127

26 https://bebrainfit.com/cognitive-costs-multitasking/

27 http://www.ucsf.edu/news/2011/04/9676/ucsf-study-multitasking-reveals-switching-glitch-aging-brain

28 https://www.ncbi.nlm.nih.gov/pubmed/26223469

29 https://bits.blogs.nytimes.com/2011/04/11/multitasking-takes-toll-on-memory-study-finds/

30 https://www.forbes.com/sites/travisbradberry/2014/10/08/multitasking- damages-your-brain-and-career-new-studies-suggest/

31 http://www.sciencedirect.com/science/article/pii/S1053811916300441

32 https://www.fastcompany.com/3057192/these-are-the-long-term-effects-of-multitasking

33 https://www.psychologytoday.com/us/blog/the-squeaky-wheel/201501/how-cellphone-use-can-disconnect-your-relationship

34 https://www.weforum.org/agenda/2016/07/multitasking-is-

exhausting-your-brain-say-neuroscientists

35 http://news.health.com/2012/10/02/many-pedestrians-hit-by-cars-are-distracted-by-mobile-devices/

36 http://www.eurekalert.org/pub_releases/2014-09/uos-bsr092314.php08/multitasking-damages-your-brain-and-career-new-studies-suggest/

37 https://www.psychologytoday.com/us/blog/the-squeaky-wheel/201606/10-real-risks-multitasking-mind-and-body

38 https://www.newyorker.com/culture/cultural-comment/a-new-theory-of-distraction

39 https://www.goodreads.com/quotes/19682-all-of-humanity-s-problems-stem-from-man-s-inability-to-sit

40 https://www.fastcompany.com/40442595/the-real-reason-why-youre-easily-distracted-has-nothing-to-do-with-technology

41 https://www.amazon.com/World-Beyond-Your-Head-Distraction/dp/0374535914

Chapter 3

1 https://medium.com/taking-note/why-deep-work-matters-in-a-distracted-world-ee4a675375f0

2 https://www.forbes.com/sites/carolinebeaton/2016/12/19/the-underlying-reason-you-cant-focus/

3 https://www.eruptingmind.com/avoidance-behaviors-and-procrastination/

4 https://www.muscleandperformance.com/training-performance/how-ali-became-the-greatest

5 https://www.ncbi.nlm.nih.gov/pubmed/26049148

6 http://blogs.discovermagazine.com/neuroskeptic/2015/06/08/brain-bigger-in-the-morning/#.W00Rny2ZOXE

7 https://www.vox.com/science-and-health/2018/2/27/17058530/sleep-night-owl-late-riser-chronotype-science-delayed-sleep-phase

8 https://www.ncbi.nlm.nih.gov/pubmed/26049148

9 http://journals.sagepub.com/doi/full/10.1177/1073858413494269

10 https://www.theguardian.com/education/2016/aug/20/does-music-really-help-you-concentrate

11 https://www.neverproductive.com/notifications/

12 http://www.nytimes.com/2007/03/25/business/25multi.html

13 https://francescocirillo.com/pages/pomodoro-technique

14 https://lifehacker.com/52-xminute-work-17-minute-break-is-the-ideal-productivi-1616541102

15 https://hbr.org/2010/05/for-real-productivity-less-is

Chapter 4

1 http://www.youtharts.ie/blog/why-creativity-important-and-what-does-it-contribute

2 https://lillstreet.com/7benefitsofcreativity

3 http://joanvinyets.net/the-importance-of-creative-intelligence-for-our-society/

4 https://www.allbusiness.com/the-importance-of-creativity-in-the-workplace-24566-1.html

5 https://quoteinvestigator.com/2014/10/26/creativity/

6 https://genius.com/Pink-floyd-shine-on-you-crazy-diamond-parts-i-v-lyrics

7 https://educateinspirechange.org/inspirational/art/society-kills-creativity-award-winning-pixar-esque-short-film/

8 http://www.alike.es

9 https://www.ted.com/talks/david_kelley_how_to_build_your_creative_confidence?language=en#t-107457

10 https://www.youtube.com/watch?v=iG9CE55wbtY

11 ibid

12 https://www.nytimes.com/2018/07/02/obituaries/gillian-lynne-choreographer-of-cats-is-dead-at-92.html

13 https://singjupost.com/schools-kill-creativity-sir-ken-robinson-transcript/?singlepage=1

14 http://www.startribune.com/prince-and-first-avenue-a-history-of-the-club-s-ties-to-its-brightest-star/377583391/

15 https://oohtoday.com/see-what-apples-billboards-are-showing-behind-the-mac/

16 https://www.cultofmac.com/447012/today-in-apple-history-heres-to-the-crazy-ones/

17 https://www.cnbc.com/2017/11/08/deutsche-bank-ceo-suggests-robots-could-replace-half-its-employees.html

18 https://www.fastcompany.com/3067279/you-didnt-see-this-coming-10-jobs-that-will-be-replaced-by-robots

19 https://hbr.org/2018/01/the-future-of-human-work-is-

imagination-creativity-and-strategy

20 https://hbr.org/2018/01/the-future-of-human-work-is-imagination-creativity-and-strategy

21 https://www.creativityatwork.com/2012/03/23/can-creativity-be-taught/

Chapter 5

1 https://people.com/celebrity/celebrate-sophia-lorens-80th-birthday-with-her-greatest-quotes/

2 https://stateoftheart.creatubbles.com/2014/10/29/can-anyone-learn-to-be-creative/

3 https://www.cbsnews.com/news/creativity-new-fountain-of-youth/

4 https://www.happyandauthentic.com/the-secret-to-unlocking-suppressed-creativity/

5 https://www.tandfonline.com/doi/abs/10.1080/17439760.2016.1257049

6 https://www.huffingtonpost.com/entry/creativity-happiness-psychology_us_58419e0ce4b0c68e0480689a

7 https://www.amazon.com/The-Wisdom-Oz-Accountability-Everything/dp/159184715X

8 https://www.waltdisney.org/blog/birth-mouse

9 https://www.learningliftoff.com/overcoming-obstacles-hard-work-and-persistence-paid-off-for-walt-disney/

10 https://listverse.com/2013/05/31/10-amazing-but-overlooked-innovations-by-walt-disney/

11 http://fortune.com/2014/12/29/disney-innovation-timeline/

12 https://disneyimaginations.com/about-imaginations/about-imagineering/

Chapter 6

1 https://www.psychologytoday.com/us/blog/the-addiction-connection/201506/whats-your-definition-happiness

2 Lyubomirsky et al., 2005

3 https://www.mindbodygreen.com/0-28409/the-pursuit-of-happiness-doesnt-actually-make-us-happy-try-this-instead.html

4 https://www.amazon.com/Authentic-Happiness-Psychology-Potential-Fulfillment/dp/0743222989/ref=sr_1_1?ie=UTF8&qid=1534104255&sr=8-1&keywords=authentic+happiness

Chapter 7

1 https://quoteinvestigator.com/2014/11/29/purpose/

2 https://scottjeffrey.com/personal-core-values/

3 https://www.cmu.edu/career/documents/my-career-path-activities/values- exercise.pdf

Chapter 8

1 https://www.youtube.com/watch?v=vBIWbV64N4I

2 https://blog.mindvalley.com/the-power-of-positive-thinking/

3 ibid

4 https://www.amazon.com/Insight-Surprising-Others-Ourselves-Answers/dp/0525573941/ref=sr_1_1?ie=UTF8&qid=1532982993&sr=8-1&keywords=tasha+eurich+insight&dpID=51KVt2GHacL&preST=_SY291_BO1,204,203,200_QL40_&dpSrc=srchash

5 https://positivepsychologyprogram.com/emotional-intelligence/le

6 https://www.amanet.org/training/articles/new-study-shows-nice-guys-finish-first.aspx?pcode=XCRP

7 https://www.flourishfoundation.org/wp-content/uploads/2014/04/KILLINGSWORTH-GILBERT-2010.pdf

8 https://www.ted.com/talks/tasha_eurich_increase_your_self_awareness_with_one_simple_fix

9 https://www.1843magazine.com/story/david-foster-wallace-in-his-own-words

Chapter 9

1 https://quoteinvestigator.com/2013/10/04/never-happened/

2 https://www.successconsciousness.com/mental-noise.htm

3 https://steptohealth.com/5-keys-calming-restless-mind-finding-internal-peace/

4 https://news.harvard.edu/gazette/story/2010/11/wandering-mind-not-a-happy-mind/

5 "Science of Happiness" page 14, Time Magazine 2015

6 https://www.psychologytoday.com/us/blog/trauma-and-hope/201801/mindfulness-and-being-present-in-the-moment

7 https://www.mindful.org/what-is-mindfulness/

8 https://beherenownetwork.com/seize-the-day-laurie-j-cameron/

9 https://ideas.ted.com/why-grown-ups-love-coloring-books-too/

10 https://www.webmd.com/balance/guide/what-is-mindfulness#1

11 https://www.psychologytoday.com/us/articles/200811/the-art-now-six-steps-living-in-the-moment

12 https://www.psychologytoday.com/us/articles/200811/the-art-now-six-steps-living-in-the-moment

13 https://www.ted.com/talks/mihaly_csikszentmihalyi_on_flow#t-330771

14 https://lateralaction.com/articles/mihaly-csikszentmihalyi/

15 https://yogainternational.com/article/view/the-real-meaning-of-meditation

16 ibid

Chapter 10

1 https://www.gatesofpower.com/single-post/2018/02/15/How-"Hustle"-Culture-is-Ruining-Your-Health

2 https://www.goodreads.com/quotes/437734-letting-go-gives-us-freedom-and-freedom-is-the-only

3 https://www.youtube.com/watch?v=BmCTQ_mkzHU

Chapter 11

1 http://www.goodreads.com/author/quotes/8164.Lewis_Carroll

2 https://www.huffingtonpost.com/helene-tragos-stelian/defining-your-lifes-purpose_b_11379968.html

3 http://fortune.com/2018/02/09/us-life-expectancy-dropped-again/

4 http://www.cbc.ca/strombo/videos/matthew-mcconaughey-alright-alright-alright-origin

5 https://www.nytimes.com/2018/07/02/obituaries/gillian-lynne-choreographer-of-cats-is-dead-at-92.html

6 http://richardleider.com/unlock-the-power-of-purpose/

7 https://www.psychologytoday.com/us/blog/out-the-darkness/201307/the-power-purpose

8 https://www.ncbi.nlm.nih.gov/pmc/articles/PMC5661934/

9 Rose, 2001

10 https://www.neuropsychotherapist.com/spirituality-as-connectedness/

11 https://quoteinvestigator.com/2016/06/22/why/

12 https://www.fastcompany.com/3026791/personal-mission-statements-of-5-famous-ceos-and-why-you-should-write-one-too

13 https://www.forbes.com/sites/drewhendricks/2014/11/10/personal-mission-statement-of-14-ceos-and-lessons-you-need-to-learn/#223083ac1e5e

14 http://motivatedonline.com/sir-richard-branson-on-a-mission-to-mentor/

15 https://www.forbes.com/profile/richard-branson/

16 https://craigsroda.com/personal-mission-statement/

17 https://www.forbes.com/sites/drewhendricks/2014/11/10/personal-mission-statement-of-14-ceos-and-lessons-you-need-to-learn/#223083ac1e5e

Chapter 12

1 https://quoteinvestigator.com/2015/02/03/you-can/

2 https://www.thesecret.tv/wp-content/uploads/2015/04/The-Science-of-Getting-Rich.pdf

3 https://www.psychologytoday.com/us/articles/200306/our-brains-negative-bias

4 https://www.tlnt.com/why-were-so-afraid-of-feedback/

5 https://www.youtube.com/watch?v=XgRlrBl-7Yg

6 https://positivepsychologyprogram.com/positive-mindset/

7 http://mindsetonline.com/

8 http://www.feedback.tips/the-right-feedback-mindset-of-managers-leaders

9 https://www.fastcompany.com/3045424/what-it-takes-to-change-your-brains-patterns-after-age-25

10 http://runwonder.com/life/science-explains-what-happens.html

11 https://www.fastcompany.com/3045424/what-it-takes-to-change-your-brains-patterns-after-age-25

12 ibid

13 https://jamesclear.com/feynman-mental-models

14 https://www.rd.com/health/wellness/morning-brain-exercises/

15 http://mj-ryan.com/blog/attitudes-of-gratitude-how-to-give-and-receive-joy-every-day-of-your-life/

16 http://www.thelawofattraction.com/what-is-the-law-of-attrac-

tion/

17 https://lifehacker.com/luck-is-what-happens-when-preparation-meets-opportunit-821189862

18 http://richardwiseman.com/resources/The_Luck_Factor.pdf

19 https://mandyharveymusic.com

20 https://www.nytimes.com/2017/06/08/arts/television/americas-got-talent-mandy-harvey-deaf-singer.html

21 https://www.youtube.com/watch?v=bRpbYKEDhOo

22 https://www.youtube.com/watch?v=bRpbYKEDhOo

23 https://www.bbc.com/news/disability-41850498

Chapter 13

1 http://www.businessdictionary.com/definition/visioning.html

2 https://www.youtube.com/watch?v=BSOJiSUI0z8

3 https://www.youtube.com/watch?v=BSOJiSUI0z8

4 https://www.zingermans.com/AboutUs.aspx

5 https://www.zingtrain.com/about-us

6 http://www.zingtrain.com/content/why-and-how-visioning-works

7 http://www.whatisavisionboard.com/Visionboard_History.html

8 https://www.themystica.com/hunting-magic/

9 https://www.huffingtonpost.com/marymorrissey/the-power-of-writing-down_b_12002348.html

10 Oettingen and Mayer; J Pers & Soc Psych, 2002

11 https://www.kent.ac.uk/careers/sk/skillsactionplanning.htm

12 https://www.smartsheet.com/develop-plan-action-free-templates

13 https://twitter.com/itswarenbuffett/status/1005200988721025025?lang=en

Chapter 14

1 https://productivephysician.com/deep-work/#Deep-Work-The-Rules

2 http://vedanta.org/become-a-monastic/

3 http://philosophicaldisquisitions.blogspot.com/2016/01/the-value-of-deep-work-and-how-to.html

4 https://www.youtube.com/watch?v=GjLan582Lgk

5 http://firstround.com/review/how-facebooks-vp-of-product-finds-focus-and-creates-conditions-for-intentional-work/

6 Ibid.

7 Cskikszentmihalyi, *Flow*, 1990, p.4

8 http://theconversation.com/free-divers-have-long-defied-science-and-we-still-dont-really-understand-how-they-go-so-deep-92690

9 http://www.guinnessworldrecords.com/news/2018/5/a-timeline-of-the-biggest-waves-surfed-as-rodrigo-koxa-sets-new-record-523752

10 https://www.independent.co.uk/sport/general/rodrigo-koxa-video-surf-biggest-wave-world-record-surfing-watch-nazare-beach-portugal-a8329466.html

11 https://www.fastcompany.com/3031052/how-to-hack-into-your-flow-state-and-quintuple-your-productivity

12 https://www.fastcompany.com/3031052/how-to-hack-into-your-flow-state-and-quintuple-your-productivity

13 https://www.ted.com/talks/mihaly_csikszentmihalyi_on_flow/transcript?language=en#t-332434

14 Csikszentmihalyi, 2002, p. 116

15 Csikszentmihalyi, 1990, p.3

16 https://en.oxforddictionaries.com/definition/autotelic

17 Cskikszentmihalyi, 1990, p.67

18 https://www.amazon.com/Disciplines-Execution-Achieving-Wildly-Important/dp/145162705X

Notes: